D1594919

DEVELOPING YOUR COMMUNICATION SKILLS in SOCIAL WORK

Sara Miller McCune founded SAGE Publishing in 1965 to support the dissemination of usable knowledge and educate a global community. SAGE publishes more than 1000 journals and over 800 new books each year, spanning a wide range of subject areas. Our growing selection of library products includes archives, data, case studies and video. SAGE remains majority owned by our founder and after her lifetime will become owned by a charitable trust that secures the company's continued independence.

Los Angeles | London | New Delhi | Singapore | Washington DC | Melbourne

3024   MT

Los Angeles | London | New Delhi
Singapore | Washington DC | Melbourne

SAGE Publications Ltd
1 Oliver's Yard
55 City Road
London EC1Y 1SP

SAGE Publications Inc.
2455 Teller Road
Thousand Oaks, California 91320

SAGE Publications India Pvt Ltd
B 1/I 1 Mohan Cooperative Industrial Area
Mathura Road
New Delhi 110 044

SAGE Publications Asia-Pacific Pte Ltd
3 Church Street
#10-04 Samsung Hub
Singapore 049483

© Paula Beesley, Melanie Watts and Mary Harrison 2018

First published 2018

Apart from any fair dealing for the purposes of research or
private study, or criticism or review, as permitted under the
Copyright, Designs and Patents Act, 1988, this publication
may be reproduced, stored or transmitted in any form, or
by any means, only with the prior permission in writing of
the publishers, or in the case of reprographic reproduction,
in accordance with the terms of licences issued by
the Copyright Licensing Agency. Enquiries concerning
reproduction outside those terms should be sent to the
publishers.

Editor: Kate Keers
Editorial assistant: Katie Rabot
Production editor: Katie Forsythe
Copyeditor: Lotika Singha
Proofreader: David Hemsley
Indexer: David Rudeforth
Marketing manager: Camille Richmond
Cover design: Wendy Scott
Typeset by C&M Digital (P) Ltd, Chennai, India
Printed in the UK

Library of Congress Control Number: 2017936254

British Library Cataloguing in Publication data

A catalogue record for this book is available from
the British Library

ISBN 978-1-4739-7586-6
ISBN 978-1-4739-7587-3 (pbk)

At SAGE we take sustainability seriously. Most of our products are printed in the UK using FSC papers and boards.
When we print overseas we ensure sustainable papers are used as measured by the PREPS grading system.
We undertake an annual audit to monitor our sustainability.

316|19

PAULA BEESLEY
MELANIE WATTS
MARY HARRISON

DEVELOPING YOUR COMMUNICATION SKILLS in SOCIAL WORK

TOURO COLLEGE LIBRARY
Midtown

WITHDRAWN

$SAGE

Los Angeles | London | New Delhi
Singapore | Washington DC | Melbourne

CONTENTS

ABOUT THE AUTHORS

Paula Beesley is a qualified social worker with a breadth of experience from over two decades of working with a wide variety of service users. Originally a child protection social worker, she has also spent time as a freelance practice educator. She is now a senior lecturer in social work at Leeds Beckett University, where her teaching and research interests are communication, skills development and placement provision.

Mary Harrison is a registered social worker and Fellow of the Higher Education Academy (HEA). She is currently a senior lecturer in social work at Leeds Beckett University. Mary qualified in 1989 and has worked as a residential worker, mental health social worker and mental health team manager. She was an approved social worker for eight years and a practice educator for over twenty years. She also worked in the voluntary sector in practice learning development. Her teaching interests include human growth and development, communication and professional skills development.

Melanie Watts is a registered social worker and Fellow of the Higher Education Academy (HEA). She is currently a senior lecturer in social work at Leeds Beckett University. She has been involved in social work education for the past eleven years. Before commencing her academic career, Melanie was a social worker in the practice area of children and families and looked-after children, and she worked in the statutory sector for nine years. Her research interests are improving outcomes for children in care, therapeutic work with children and young people, and decision making in child protection practice.

ACKNOWLEDGEMENTS

Paula would like to thank her wonderful husband Ade, who practises his listening skills every day to support her, and her children, Lily and James, who have been enthusiastic throughout.

Mary would like to thank all the colleagues she has worked with over the years from backgrounds other than social work and who have been such a support and inspiration.

Melanie would like to thank her family and partner Steven for their encouragement and continued support.

We would like to collectively thank Kate for giving us the opportunity and support to create this book, and to our team, who are so positive about achieving anything and making us believe that this book was possible.

Paula, Mary and Melanie

INTRODUCTION

The introduction will define social work communication and discuss its importance to effective social work practice. It will take into account the significance and consequences of inadequate communication by social workers by drawing on historical concerns and research. It will also reflect on the modern context of skills development within the Health and Care Professions Council's *Guidance on Conduct and Ethics for Students* (HCPC, 2016a), the British Association of Social Workers' *Professional Capability Framework* (BASW, 2016), and the government's Knowledge and Skills Statements (KSS). The learning features present throughout the book will be introduced, followed by a summary of each chapter.

THE NEED FOR COMMUNICATION

This book does not need to re-hash past tragedies. The histories of Daniel Pelka, Victoria Climbié, Baby Peter, and many more, tell their own stories and are entrenched in our professional history. But the common thread in all these tragedies appears to be the breakdown in communication at some level, be it with parents or between professionals. However, examples of poor communication still circulate: McNicoll (2016) reported in *Community Care* on the outcome of AS *v* TH (False Allegations of Abuse), where the judge concluded that the social worker had neither challenged the mother's perspective nor utilised open questions, and consequently, had not begun to listen to the father's perspective. The judge raised a high level of concern that the recording did not accurately and objectively reflect the facts of the case, and that poor communication between the professionals resulted in repetition of work. However, the word *extraordinary* was used by the children's guardian to describe the poor quality of work: an indication that this is not the norm. For each tragedy that makes the headlines, and we – quite correctly – hang our heads in sadness and shame for our profession, we should also be proud of the high quality of communication that the numerous social workers in the country display on a daily basis. Healy et al. (2016) highlight that even in complex situations where service users are reluctant to engage, good communication and engaging the service user in the process enhance outcomes.

Communication is a two-way process. It involves two (or more) people interacting to exchange information and views. Communication can be seen to be like a game of table tennis or ping-pong: the social worker (server) begins the conversation with an explanation or question that requires the other person, the service user, to respond (hit the ping-pong ball back); the conversation continues with active listening, open questions and clarification by the social worker and information sharing by the service user (stimulating a volley of conversation). If the communication is just a monologue, it will fall flat like a ping-pong ball flying across the table. Communication requires both parties to interact to ensure it is effective.

Without communication, we are unable to understand the other person's viewpoint, and we are unable to let people know our own. Social work is about understanding that everyone will have a unique perspective and that often it is about listening to each and every involved person's wishes, feelings, opinions, needs and values, gathering that information, and making a decision based on the complexities of competing needs. It is rare that social work will have a simple outcome that neatly resolves all issues and priorities. Instead, social work is often a complicated task of communication and negotiation around ethical dilemmas.

As a profession, social work has its own identity. At time of writing we are registered with the HCPC. However, the Children and Social Work Bill 2016 puts social work practice and education at the forefront of government scrutiny and it is likely that a new social work accrediting body will be formed in the future. Regardless of the accrediting body involved, social workers are expected to act in a certain way: with proficiency and professionalism. The second standard of the HCPC's (2016a) *Guidance on Conduct and Ethics for Student* states that all professionals must *communicate appropriately and effectively*. This demonstrates the importance that communication has in developing professionalism.

The now defunct College of Social Work developed a professional standards framework, the Professional Capability Framework (PCF), under which nine domains were created, in which as a social worker you will need to demonstrate progression throughout your career. The PCF has been adopted and updated by BASW (2016), and you will need to familiarise yourself with the domain criteria for your level of social work. Supplementary to the PCF are the KSS published by the Department for Education (2016) and Department of Health (2015) for children's and adults social workers, respectively. These provide clear and specific statements on the expectations of a social worker. As with the PCF criteria, you will need to familiarise yourself with the KSS, in which you will see that communication skills and good relationships underpin the work and are seen as critical in any social worker's career.

Throughout the book, you will be asked to reflect on how your skills are meeting the PCF and KSS, so that you develop your understanding of them.

VALUES IN SOCIAL WORK COMMUNICATION

Power involves the potential to control and restrict, to form and transform. (Fook, 2016: 70).

Social work carries a high level of power: you can remove a child from their family, decree that an unaccompanied minor is not the age that they claim and therefore not entitled to services, or commit someone to mental health treatment against their wishes. Clearly, it is imperative that the decisions you make are fully informed decisions, which can only be made if you have asked open questions, actively listened, clarified and challenged. Fook (2016) argues that decisions can be made in partnership with service users, empowering the service user with the social worker's power. However, social work communication is not just for the big decisions, it is at the heart of every part of our practice. In our everyday interactions with service users and professionals, we should practise good quality communication skills to ensure that every decision we make reflects the wishes and feelings of our service user and takes into account all relevant information.

As we will discuss in Chapter Three (Listening), person-centred practice should be at the heart of your social work communication. Person-centred practice is, as the phrase suggests, when the service user is put at the centre of our practice. The service user's wishes and feelings should be sought and heard, their history acknowledged and utilised, and their perspective on solutions harnessed as a positive. The phrase 'seeing the service user as the expert in themselves' springs to mind. They know about their own strengths and weaknesses: your role as social worker is to support them to identify those strengths and weaknesses and support them to develop by seeing them from a wider, objective context. Communication is the key to achieving this role.

Different service users and professionals will have different perspectives and priorities. For example, Ofsted (2015a,b) undertook two surveys, one with young people looked after by a local authority and one with the adults involved (both parents and professionals), and which looked at their perspectives of social care. The survey of adults (Ofsted, 2015a) concluded that better communication would enhance the social worker's practice. It identified two key communications themes: ensuring that information was shared, and that the adults' perspective was sought and heard. The young people's survey (Ofsted, 2015b) identified that they wanted to be able to talk about their feelings and problems. This example illustrates how different service user groups have different priorities: the young people wanted a confidant, whilst the adults wanted to be informed and involved. The important lesson here is that, as a social worker, you do not assume that you know what a service user wants, but right from the start you listen to their perspective to ensure that you are engaging them and meeting their needs.

Partnership is a commonly used term within social work to imply that a social worker is seeking the wishes and feelings of a service user, and that the service user will be involved in the decision-making process about matters that will affect them. The principle is that if you *empower* a service user to make a decision with you, they will be more capable of making a decision without support next time. Also, they will have ownership of the decision and thus will be more likely to engage with the process. Partnership can only be achieved by open and honest communication with a service user to understand their perspective and ensure that they are informed about the interventions that will happen.

Trevithick (2012) reflects that a service user will engage with the social worker who appears to be committed and caring. Such engagement will empower the service user to feel optimistic about change and therefore more likely to initiate and evidence the change. Hennessey (2011) argues that social work is fundamentally about the relationship between service user and social worker. He further argues that the relationship is inevitably impacted by social policy, legislation, procedures, societal construction of the issues that are affecting the service user, as well as the values the social worker holds, the past and current experiences of the service user, and each of their personalities. The social worker's *self* engages the service user through showing that they too are human. This book will encourage you to work from a relationship-based perspective.

Communication should be undertaken with consideration of your social work values as set out in the HCPC's (2016a) *Guidance on Conduct and Ethics for Students*. However, you will also need to understand how service users are oppressed. Thompson's (1997) personal, cultural and societal (PCS) model enables you to look at how a service user is oppressed on each of these levels. Whilst this book does not include a detailed discussion of the social construction of the oppression of service users, it is helpful to understand what may have impacted on the individual service user and how it may influence their communication and interaction with you. For example, on a home visit a young father, Joel, answers the door. You explain that you have come to undertake a duty visit for a colleague, but Joel becomes verbally aggressive, shouting that he does not wish to talk to you and insisting that you leave. It may be that this young father was looked after by the local authority as a child, and has a history of a progression of social workers making false promises and then leaving their role, which might make him feel apprehensive about talking to you and he does not trust a new face.

The personal level: Joel feels disabled and despondent by his lack of chances in life as a result of being a looked-after child, and that he has a poorer chance of obtaining the employment he would like as he did not achieve in school.

The cultural level: Joel is housed in poor-quality accommodation, as continual budget cuts and housing policies have reduced publicly funded social housing. This is the only accommodation the housing department could allocate him and his ten-month-old son. Thus he feels embarrassed to show you the flat, which he cannot afford to furnish as he spends his limited benefit income on nappies and baby food.

The structural level: Each of these factors impact on Joel's less-than-welcoming response to you. Your role as an emotionally intelligent student social worker is to have empathy for how he is feeling and attempt to engage him to show that you are both non-judgemental and supportive of his situation.

Your communication will need to take into account a wide variety of variables, and be flexible and responsive to the needs of the service user. This book will help you to develop a communication skills toolkit, from which you are able to utilise a range of responses depending on the situation and the service user's needs.

PROFESSIONAL IDENTITY

It is clear that as a social worker, you cannot work as an automaton. If you were to follow procedure and theory to the letter, without putting your *self* into the working relationship, you would appear uncaring and soulless. This is not to say that you should throw away the procedural handbook or work outside of social work methodology, but that by undertaking the intervention with your own strengths, and with regard to the service user as an individual, you can go to develop a relationship that is supportive, flexible and productive. Levy et al. (2014) discuss that an individual social worker's professional identity is shaped by personal values, professional values, emotional resilience (they call it coherence) and emotional intelligence (they call it self-differentiation) and empathic skills, and is further influenced by external factors such a quality of support and supervision and social work role stress levels. Indeed, Ingram (2015) reflects that a social worker's professional identity is made up of culturally agreed, or socially constructed, norms: that is, the values, behaviours and skills that are common to all social workers.

However, we argue that this should be supplemented with your own personality. There is no point in being a 'loud' a social worker if you are naturally quiet. A service user will not feel that you are natural if you are trying to act in a proscribed way, and will doubt your honesty and openness. This book will encourage you to take your personal strengths and develop and utilise them to engage the service user as well as other professionals and your peers, effectively. Miehls and Moffatt (2000) argued that your professional identity would be enhanced as you reflect on and understand your communication and interactions within an intervention, all of which will hone your emotional intelligence (see Chapter One).

LEARNING FEATURES

Throughout this book, there are a variety of learning features: exercises for you to complete to support your communication skills development. There will, inevitably, be some exercises that you engage with more than others. Thus you do not need to undertake every single exercise in the book in chronological order. Instead we have provided learning features that you can choose to utilise as dictated by your individual needs. The learning features are as follows.

> *Links to Knowledge and Skills Statements*: Each chapter begins with a link to both the children's and adult's KSS (Department of Health, 2015; Department of Education, 2016) to enable you to understand clearly how the chapter links to the expected roles of the social worker.

> *Activity*: You will be given an activity to undertake that will apply the communication skill discussed in the chapter to your everyday communication. By reflecting on your non-social work communications, you will begin to understand how you respond to incidents and people.

> *Case study*: You will be given brief facts about a social work scenario, and asked to reflect on your responses to it. This will enable you to apply your developing communications skills to social work interventions, which will develop your professional identity.

> *Reflective task*: You will be asked to reflect on a dilemma or issue, to further your understanding of the communication skill. The methods of reflection recommended in Chapter One will enable you to reflect on why you communicate in the way you do and determine an action plan to develop your communication skills further.

> *Communication skills audit*: At the end of each chapter, you will be asked to make a final reflection on your skills development from the topic of that chapter. It is recommended that you use the other learning features in each chapter to enhance your understanding of your skills and areas to develop as well one of the reflective models from the chapter to audit your communication skills. The communication skills audit will be based on the PCF domains (BASW, 2016), and will ask you to reflect on your strengths in regard to a number of the domains and your identified areas for development. You will then be asked to complete an action plan to develop your skills. Two or three points will be the most you need to undertake. Make sure that the action points are SMART, to ensure that they are Small, achievable, realistic targets to motivate you to action the proposed changes. The first communication skills audit at the end of Chapter One provides examples to help you begin your regular reflection.

> *Further reading*: Suggestions will be provided to enable you to explore the communication skill further.

The HCPC's (2016b) *Standards of Conduct, Performance and Ethics* requires that qualified social workers *maintain and develop their knowledge and skills*. By using the learning features and completing a communication skills audit at this stage in your career you will be embracing a practice requirement that will then embedded into your practice throughout your career.

CHAPTER SUMMARIES

Each chapter will take an integrated approach and include four main aspects of the communication area being discussed:

- The communication skills theory behind the communications area. This will be underpinned with reference to social work values, relevant legislation, social policy and/or procedures, etc., as social work communication cannot be seen in isolation.
- Learning features that ask the reader to reflect on and develop their skills and areas for development, perspective and values. These include a wide range of examples, and thus cover working with a wide variety of user groups and issues.
- Discussion of the communication skills within the area. As you will see in the next chapter, the emphasis is not on having a right response, but about thinking about a number of styles to enable you to become responsive and flexible, and to develop your own style of social work communication.
- The communication skill under discussion will be mapped against the PCF and KSS. This will support your development of understanding of these requirements.

Chapter One: Reflection and emotional intelligence

Chapter One will consider student reflection and its impact on skill development. You will be asked to think about the conscious competency matrix to ensure that you understand that thought needs to go beyond your initial response to your ability. Reflective models will be considered, including Gibbs' reflective cycle and Schön's 'reflection in and on action'. The chapter will introduce you to the concept of emotional intelligence and discuss how your emotions and your understanding of the service user's emotions will impact on your ability to communicate.

Chapter Two: Initial engagement

Chapter Two will reflect on the importance for social workers of initial engagement with service users, and the skills required to do this effectively and efficiently. It will explore the service user's perspective within an initial engagement and explore how social workers can empathise with a service user's recent and historical history to anticipate and plan for different responses. The chapter will continue with the practical planning before meeting a service user, and finish with consideration of the practical issues that a social worker needs to consider in their initial engagement with a service user.

Chapter Three: Listening

Chapter Three will consider the importance of listening and the skills of listening. It will also explore the skills of silence, non-verbal listening, attending, active listening, minimal encouragers and checking understanding. You will be asked to undertake exercises that reflect on your personal and professional listening skills, and help you recognise the areas that you need to develop. The chapter will conclude with a reflection on the social work communication skills that are needed when a service user's limited communication or coherence impacts on your ability to listen.

Chapter Four: Clarification

Chapter Four will focus on the importance of clarifying details and information relayed by service users and professionals to ensure that misunderstandings do not occur. It will discuss how to use open versus closed questions, paraphrasing, mirroring and summarising. It will ask the reader to reflect on congruence of verbal and non-verbal communication, and how to clarify this with a service user. The chapter will also reflect on ensuring that, as a communicator, you achieve clarity of information for those with whom you communicate.

Chapter Five: Empathy

Chapter Five will consider empathic communication. This chapter will first seek to ensure that the reader understands the difference between empathy and sympathy, and the important role that empathy plays in engaging clients. Next, it will critically analyse how you can ensure that the service user is valued and validated whilst working with a social worker. The chapter will conclude with a reflection on the impact of being empathic as well as on emotional intelligence, and the need for the reader to ensure that they are proactive in remaining emotionally well.

Chapter Six: Challenging: holding sensitive conversations

Chapter Six describes when and why a social worker needs to challenge a service user, and when not to do so. It will ask the reader to reflect on the appropriateness of challenging, and on the positivity of risk-taking. The chapter will offer advice on how to challenge assertively and ask the reader to think about the effectiveness of stimulating change rather than demanding change. This will include both when and how to give constructive feedback to service users to ensure it is heard effectively. The chapter will discuss professional roles and boundaries to support the reader's understanding.

Chapter Seven: Working with resistance

Firstly, Chapter Seven will reflect on causal factors why some service users are difficult to engage or display conflict or resistance. It will discuss the difference between reluctance and resistance and the need for social worker understanding and empathy to engage the service user. The chapter will then consider techniques to work with conflict or resistance, including assertiveness, negotiation skills, and consider the appropriateness of an authoritative approach. The chapter will end by returning to the subject of emotional intelligence and the use of supervision when dealing with resistance and/or conflict.

Chapter Eight: Barriers to effective communication

Chapter Eight will critically analyse the issues that impede our communication. It will go through areas covered in the other chapters and consider the issues that restrict or prevent our communication, for example, the physical issues, the impact of our emotional competence, or social barriers. Although this book is primarily focused on what you can do – a strengths-based perspective on developing your communication skills – this chapter focuses more on what you should not do.

Chapter Nine: Written communication: case recording, letters, texts, social media

Chapter Nine will ask the reader to reflect on the importance of prompt and appropriate recording, and put this into a procedural context. It will discuss different styles of communication that are required when utilising written communication, including texts, letters and social media. It will offer the student direction on effective writing, and ask them to reflect on their written skills audit.

Chapter Ten: Assessment and report writing: critical analysis

Chapter Ten will describe assessment styles, and ask the reader to reflect on their preferred style within Smale et al.'s (1993) models of assessment, and explain how to follow Sutton's (1994) ASPIRE model (assessment, planning, intervention, review and evaluation) of assessment. It will discuss evidence-based assessment writing to support an analytical perspective. It will emphasise person-centred assessment writing and ensuring that service users are aware of and understand content. It will conclude by looking at reports and chronologies.

Chapter Eleven: Inter-professional communication

Chapter Eleven will consider the importance of multi-agency and inter-professional working from a legal and social policy perspective, and highlight the positive impact on interventions of good communication between agencies. It will tackle the need for the balancing act between diplomacy, assertiveness and tact within individual communications and within more formal meeting settings. Students will be asked to reflect on their confidence in this area and support their development. The chapter will also critically analyse the impact on the service user of the power differential when professionals are communicating with each other about them, rather than with them.

Chapter Twelve: Managing endings

Chapter Twelve will discuss how the reader can disengage from service users, both in the context of the intervention ending, and in the context of a case transfer. It will also reflect on ending individual appointments or meetings assertively and clearly. It will encourage the reader to routinely clarify, summarise and confirm achievements and positives as they move forward. The chapter will also ask the reader to critically analyse endings that do not feel positive, and the impact on the social worker's self and the service user, by referring again to emotional intelligence. It will also consider the emotional impact on the service user within endings.

CONCLUSION

The philosophy behind this book is to motivate you, the social work student, to reflect on your communication skills, your strengths and areas for development. However, a word of caution is merited: you will benefit from this book only as much as you are prepared to put into it. We have provided the theory and practice ideas in relation to communication skills, and learning features to stimulate reflection, but you will need to engage with these features in an open and honest way to maximise your development as you progress through the book. You are encouraged to develop long-term unconscious reflexivity on your practice, and to embrace the social work concept of perpetual skill enhancement.

REFLECTION AND EMOTIONAL INTELLIGENCE

Links to Knowledge and Skills Statements

Adults: critical reflection and analysis; organisational context; professional ethics

Children's: relationships and effective direct work; communication; role of supervision; organisational context

INTRODUCTION

This chapter will consider student reflection and its impact on skill development. You will be asked to think about the conscious competency matrix to ensure that you understand that thought needs to go beyond your initial response to your ability. Reflective models will be considered, including Gibbs' reflective cycle, and Schön's reflection in and on action. The chapter will introduce you to the concept of emotional intelligence and how your emotions and your understanding of the service user's emotions will impact on your ability to communicate.

REFLECTION

A basic tenet of social work practice is that you should always reflect on your practice, and aim to enhance and develop your knowledge and skills. Ingram (2015) argues that reflection should also include an understanding of our emotional response. In any situation, you will need to reflect on why it happened and what could have been different if it were to happen again, so that if it did happen again, there would be a(n even) better outcome. As a social worker we should never feel safe that we know how to be a social worker, as at that point we are no longer a good social worker. We should continually be learning about new legislation, theory and procedures, and we should also be constantly adapting and enhancing our practice to meet the individual service user's needs and ensuring that we practise in our best possible way. As a student social worker, you should aim to reflect on all events, to evaluate and enhance your practice. This can be undertaken after a home visit or meeting or on the commute home. You should consider your practice, the impact of your *self* on others, the actions of service users and colleagues, and the impact of contemporary challenges such as oppression, social policy and legislation on your practice. Bassot (2016) suggests that reflection utilises a *metaphorical mirror*, whereby the reflector utilises a range of different mirrors to enable them to see an intervention from several angles or perspectives. This will enable greater understanding of the interventions that you undertake and the service users with whom you work.

Students can initially often find it difficult to decide what to reflect upon. In order to avoid the choice of content becoming a stressful preventive factor, we advise that the written reflection content should be the incident that is still making you think as you leave placement for the day, as that is the one that has intrigued, upset or pleased you. The 'chore' of writing reflections can also be preventative, so ensure that you see it as a learning task – as important as attending lectures or undertaking an assessment. If you allow yourself fifteen minutes a day to reflect, it will become part of your routine and easier to undertake as you develop your reflective muscle.

Reflection is entrenched in policy for social workers as Health and Care Professions Council (HCPC) registration requires that we demonstrate continuous professional development (CPD). Similarly, reflection is entrenched in the British Association of Social Workers Professional Capability Framework (PCF; BASW, 2016), which expects continual development as your career progresses. Reflection has its own domain in the PCF – Domain 6, critical reflection.

> Social workers are knowledgeable about and apply the principles of critical thinking and reasoned discernment. They identify, distinguish, evaluate and integrate multiple sources of knowledge and evidence. These include practice evidence, their own practice experience, service user and carer experience together with research-based, organisational, policy and legal knowledge. They use critical thinking augmented by creativity and curiosity.
> (BASW, 2016)

ACTIVITY 1.1

Write a 300–500 word reflection on a conversation that you had with someone this morning.

- Think about briefly describing who said and did what.
- Think about why you and they may have said and done those things.
- What communication strengths did you use?
- What communication skills could you have used differently?

With this exercise, we are asking you to begin to undertake your communication skills audit. As you progress through this book you will be asked at every juncture to reflect on which communication skills that you possess and which you need to develop further.

ACTIVITY 1.2

Ask the person you were talking to:

- What did they think of your communication strengths and areas to develop?

Did the person mention anything that surprised you? The conscious competency matrix (Figure 1.1) asks you to think about where you are in your skills audit. There will be skills that you know that you can do well, which is when you are consciously conscious of your skill, and skills that you know that you need to develop further, when you are consciously incompetent. In many ways these are the easy skills: you are aware of your strengths and area of development. But throughout this book, we will ask you to reflect further and start to identify those communications skills in which you may be unconsciously incompetent: those that you do not know you need

Unconscious incompetence: You don't know you don't have the skill	Conscious incompetence: You know that you don't have the skill
Unconscious competence: You do the skill well without thinking about it	Conscious competence: You are aware that the skill is one of your strengths

Figure 1.1 Conscious competency matrix (source unknown).

to develop. By asking your partner in the conversation, you may begin to identify communication skills that you were not aware that you needed to develop.

When using this book and reflecting on your communication skills, it may be helpful to be aware of your preferred method of learning to enhance your development. There are a number of questionnaires that enable you to do this. For example, VARK (Fleming, 1987), which stands for Visual, Aural, Read-write and Kinaesthetic, or Honey and Mumford's (1982) Activist, Theorist, Pragmatist and Reflector learning styles. These may help you to understand the best way for you to learn: if you are a reflector the reflective exercises may be more beneficial than reading the theory. However, we cannot but raise a word of caution at this point: just because you prefer one way of learning, do not ignore the rest. At this stage, you should be strengthening your learning in your weaker areas. An active learner who ignores theory and fails to reflect does not develop themselves and may end up as unconsciously incompetent. Ingram (2015) reminds us Schön (1983) stated that in order to reflect effectively, you have to apply the theories to understand why things happened. He argued that to just be a reflector was impossible, you have to action your conclusions.

HOW TO REFLECT

There are many ways to reflect. As discussed above, you should aim to develop the reflective skills that enable you to reflect quietly as you finish a home visit, commute or write an assessment. However, when first starting to reflect, it can be helpful to have a structure to work within and a common way to achieve this is by utilising a written exercise. Indeed, many social work courses require the social work student to write regular reflections, and it is likely that your university will have a proforma for you to complete, which will guide you through your reflection with prompts and/or questions. When undertaking the reflective exercises in this book, consider using one of the following formats initially to aid your focus.

The simplest one is Driscoll's (2007) What? model, which suggests the following format:

What? Describe briefly the incident

So What? Why you think this may have happened

Now What? What can you learn from this incident

Gibbs (1988) proposes a reflective cycle to reflect within (Figure 1.2). This can be helpful as it can facilitate understanding of the steps that are necessary to go through to reflect effectively:

Description: The reflective cycle begins with a brief description. When many students begin to write they spend much time telling us about what they did. Try to develop a clear, concise writing style so that you briefly tell the reader the most important facts. Chapter Nine discusses concise writing for recording purposes: the skills you need are transferable and development of one benefits the other. A reflection should be no more than 500 words long: it is not an

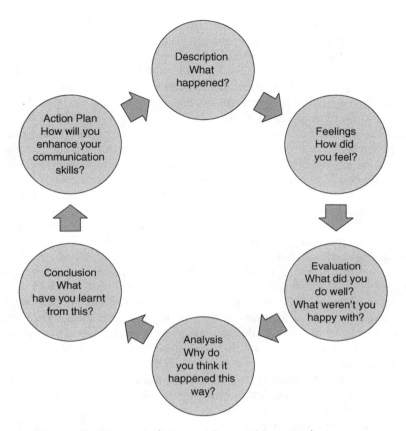

Figure 1.2 Gibbs' reflective cycle (adapted from Gibbs, 1988)

assignment but a reflection to support you to develop. This means that your description cannot exceed 100 words. Give it a try: it's hard! And remember, you do not always have to write: a pictorial representation can work well too. The important task is to think about and reflect on the incident.

Feelings: At this point you should think about how the discussion made you feel: happy, sad, upset, angry, elated, disappointed, neutral. It may be that you are experiencing a variety of feelings. Howe (2008) reminds us that we can have 'multiple, contrasting, even conflicting emotions', and points out that awareness of this is one element of our emotional intelligence.

Evaluation: Now you should start to reflect. What elements of the discussion were you happy with? What did you say that afterwards made you smile? But equally, were there elements that you would have liked to communicate differently? Did you say anything that makes you squirm? Whilst you are now reflecting, you are evaluating *how* you did, not reflecting on the why.

Analysis: It is here that you start to think about the why. You will need to critically reflect on your contribution to the incident. What issues may have impacted on the quality of your communication? Your existing (or lack of) relationship with the service user can cause or ease anxiety, your emotional and physical health will affect your ability to process and express your thoughts, and external issues (a heated row with a friend, a need to understand the topic for your assignment, concentrating too hard on saying the right thing, etc.; see Chapter Seven) will all impact on your ability to communicate. However, you will also need to reflect on your existing communication skills and areas to develop, and utilise the conscious competence model to reflect if there are areas that you are becoming aware of as you progress through the book (which, of course, the minute you become aware of them are no longer unconscious incompetent areas, but now conscious incompetent areas, and hopefully will progress into conscious competence by the end of the book). It can be helpful for some people to draw a spider diagram to help them think about the issues that may be impacting on their communication.

You will be required at this stage to utilise theory to help you to understand the why, in this case the communication skills theory that we will draw on throughout the book. Knott (2013) calls this being an informed reflective practitioner. Without drawing on theory, it becomes impossible to understand why things work or how they could be enhanced. You may need to reflect on whether you have communicated in an anti-oppressive manner, and whether your values have impacted on your communication. Further thought should also be given as to whether your agency's philosophy or procedures, or legislative criteria, have influenced your ability to communicate. Knott (2013) reminds you to reflect on the ethical issues that arise: for example, your agency's needs and the service user's needs may differ: how do you balance those needs? You may also need to reflect on the social construction of the service user's response. Fook (2016) recommends reflection on the impact of social structures and oppression on the service user: why does the person behave and respond in the way that they do? What influences have led to this?

If you are reflecting within the PCF and/or the Knowledge and Skills Statement (for adults or children), you would also consider in this section the domains you had met and those you need to develop further. The analysis section should be the longest and most detailed section of your reflection, as it requires you to think of layers of issues. This means that one issue can never explain a situation, as many factors will contribute to an outcome. The role of the reflector is to identify some of these contributing factors and explore their influence.

But remember, there is no right or wrong at this point (other than gross misconduct or oppressive practice). There will be many reasons why something happens, and it will be impossible to identify each and every one to pinpoint the cause. The idea is for you to reflect on possibilities of why, but not for you to identify areas for development or to apportion blame.

Conclusion: Here you will summarise your communication skills audit, your communication skills strengths and areas to develop.

Action plan: And finally, you will give yourself one to three action points that you will take into your next discussion with your tutor or practice educator, which will enhance your communication with them. Gardener (2014) argues that as a reflective student social worker you will need to be open and creative. This means that when thinking of an action plan for developing your practice, you will need to be open to change as well as open to creative and flexible ways to enhance your skills.

We have just worked through each step of Gibbs' reflective cycle. Now consider it in practice. Below is Aisha's reflection based on a home visit she undertook on her placement.

CASE STUDY 1.1

DESCRIPTION

I am two weeks into my first placement in a child protection team. I accompanied a social worker on a home visit. I was anxious to make a good impression, but ended up sharing personal information about myself from when I had had a similar experience.

FEELINGS

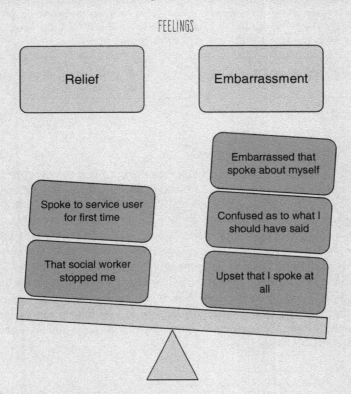

Figure 1.3 Balancing complex feelings

(Continued)

(Continued)

I am feeling very confused right now. I feel elated: I spoke to a service user for the first time. But I feel devastated because it was a disaster. I just wanted to disappear into the settee when I started talking about myself, but I just couldn't stop myself.

EVALUATION

Table 1.1   Example of possible thoughts when reflecting on practice

Positives	What went wrong
I was dressed professionally, my phone was turned off, I felt prepared.	I shared personal information about my history with the service user and the social worker.
I watched how the social worker spoke to the service user. She had a relaxed but clear manner. I will try to use that when I speak to service users.	I was not clear on the purpose of the visit: I was so excited to be going on my first home visit that I rushed into it without discussion.
In the car on the way back, I was able to tell the social worker I was sorry.	I was very anxious to do well, and concentrated so much on that that I lost concentration.

ANALYSIS

So why did I blurt that out? Well, the service user struck some chords with me: similar age, similar story, even similar name! Reflecting back, I can see that I over-identified with the service user. But in some ways, I was also feeling a little bit 'safe'. I liked the colleague I was out with. We had been chatting about our interests, life plan, etc. I can see now that boundaries are really important in social work (Domain 1: Professionalism). Henderson and Mathew-Bryne (2016) recognise that having different personal and professional boundaries are very important for any social worker, but it is especially hard for student social workers to get the balance right. That made me feel better: that it is okay to get it wrong, that learning from this is what is important. I am beginning to see that service users aren't my friends, or my peers. I am here to help them, so I need to be friendly, yet not too personal. Not an easy line to walk, but I am going to try (Domain 6: Critical reflection).

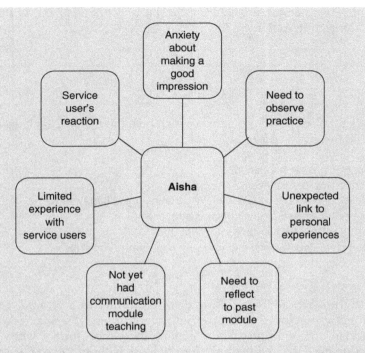

Figure 1.4 Example of spider diagram of contributing factors that impact on intervention

CONCLUSION

I feel that although I shared information inappropriately with the service user by interrupting the social worker's intervention, that I have been able to reflect on my reasons for doing so. I need to develop understanding on the importance of professional boundaries, and an ability to adhere to them.

ACTION PLAN

1. Seek university counselling to address personal issues.
2. Talk to practice educator about how I felt, the impact of the visit on the service user, and if this impacts on my placement.
3. Talk to practice educator about coping strategies to help me if this situation arose again.

Now consider how you can use Gibbs' reflective cycle to reflect on your own experiences by completing Activity 1.3.

ACTIVITY 1.3

Think back to your reflection on a conversation from this morning. Do it again using Gibbs' reflective model below:

- Description: What happened?
- Feelings: How did you feel?
- Evaluation: What did you do well? What weren't you happy with?
- Analysis: Why do you think it happened this way?
- Conclusion: What have you learnt from this?
- Action plan: How will you enhance your communication skills?

It is beneficial to start reflecting using these proformas as a prompt, and in time it will become instinctive to reflect on all interventions you undertake. As your journey through the book progresses, initially use Gibbs' format when undertaking a reflection exercise, and then begin to practise without the proforma. As your reflection skills progress, it is likely that you will find Gibbs' model simplistic. It is worth remembering Kolb (originally 1984, reviewed in 2015) recommends a model in which to undertake the reflection on action that is widely used. It is based on the same principles, but that as a reflector you move through concrete experience, where you might undertake communication with a service user or professional; then undertake reflective observation, where you reflect on the communication skills that you have used; then turn to abstract conceptualisation, thinking about your strengths and areas for development; and finally undertaking active experimentation, where you try different communication styles to see which suit you and the service user's needs. It may be that you find this model more useful as you progress.

Another reflective model is that of Schön's (1983) reflection in action and on action. He argues that when you are in the middle of an intervention you will be reflecting *in action*: making rapid reflections that inform your responses and interventions. Many of the chapters in this book will require you, whilst practising the communication skill, to reflect and respond whilst in action. For example, when listening to a service user you will be required to undertake active listening: reflecting on all the verbal and non-verbal communication that you receive whilst also filtering possible coping strategies behind presenting behaviour, and yet also applying relevant legislation, agency policy and theory. Fook (2016) refers to this as *reflexive* practice, and recognises it is a complex and difficult practice, but that beginning with reflective practice you will become more reflexive, therefore enhancing your interventions.

REFLECTIVE TASK 1.1

Arrange to have coffee with a fellow social work student. During the conversation, actively reflect on your use of your communication skills (consciously be aware of your competence (skills) and incompetence (areas to develop)) and reflect on your peer's responses.

Schön (1983) recommends that after the intervention you reflect further on the issues discussed whilst in action, but also reflect on your own practice. What did you do well, what practice could you enhance? You can utilise the written reflective models at this point to aid your *on action* reflection.

REFLECTIVE TASK 1.2

After you have finished your coffee and left your peer, reflect further: what issues affected the way you communicated? (Location, your relationship with your peer, your emotional or physical wellbeing that day, etc.?) Could you have communicated differently at any point?

We often say that retrospection is a wonderful thing. It can be easy to say this is what I would have done when not in the heat of the moment, influenced by a range of factors. But in Schön's reflection model's case, retrospection *is* a wonderful thing. Schön (1983) asks you to look back, to be retrospective, not to judge and lay blame, but to learn from the experience and enhance your future practice.

Gardener (2014) recommends that you should develop from seeing reflection as a chore, when you write a reflection for a module or for placement demands, to seeing it as a natural and positive part of your practice. Once you understand the process of reflecting utilising written formats, you will become adept at reflecting on your own. Many social workers reflect automatically (unconsciously competently), immediately after every visit that they undertake. They will think about why the service user acted in the way that they did, and how their responses impacted on the assessment of the situation. They will reflect on how they intervened with and responded to the service user, what they did well, and how they could enhance their practice further.

Qualified social workers will access reflective support in supervision, where they can discuss the case and their interventions to reflect to ensure that they are making the best decision for the service user. The Knowledge and Skills Statement for adults (Department of Health, 2015) has critical reflection as a clear component in Section 8, which recommends the use of supervision to enable and develop reflection on case work. Whilst the Knowledge and Skills Statement for children (Department for Education, 2016) does not have a section called reflection, it is clearly incorporated into the equivalent section, Section 10, on supervision. As a social work student on placement, you should expect a strong level of reflective practice from your practice educator. Scragg (2014) reminds us that your practice educator will be skilled at reflection and will help you to develop your reflective skills in supportive supervision, where you can explore areas of development. Scragg also reminds you to advocate if you are not receiving this. Ingram (2015) reiterates that social workers have professional norms, which will vary from team to team and agency to agency. However, it is acceptable to demand time to reflect even in a team that does not see reflection as part of the team's identity, as it is entrenched in our national professional identity through the HCPC, PCF and the Knowledge and Skills Statement.

HOW TO ACCEPT FEEDBACK

The process of this book is about developing your communication skills through self-awareness through reflection. However, it is also very useful, although difficult, to receive, hear and utilise feedback from others. Many of the activities throughout the book will ask you to think about how you feel about interventions, but some will ask you to ask the person involved for feedback. As you progress as a student social worker, you will benefit from feedback from your practice educator, colleagues and service users with whom you work.

When receiving feedback, the important issue is not to take the criticism personally. It is likely that whilst you will receive positive comments you will also receive constructive criticism, in order to help you identify your areas for development. If these are provided using evidence-based explanations, then you can reflect on the described incident using one of the reflective styles described above. This should help you to identify why the person made their comments and to develop an action plan to enhance your communication skills. It is the other person's reflective opinion on your communication skills, and you must filter this opinion by considering whether it is objective and relevant. You do not have take every negative comment to heart, yet be open to hearing the need to develop your communication skills.

EMOTIONAL INTELLIGENCE

Emotional intelligence is a combination of your understanding of your own emotional wellbeing, an awareness of how you are feeling at that time and your more consistent strengths and areas of development, and an awareness of the person with whom you are talking, be it service user, peer, professional or supervisor (social awareness). Goleman (1995) argued that emotional intelligence is made up of self-awareness, self-management, social awareness and relationship management. This means that it is not just awareness, but a conscious adjustment to enable optimum communication given Goleman's factors. Grant et al. (2014) argue that your self-awareness and social awareness enable you to manage the emotional complexities of communication, which will help you problem solve and thus support service users' progress and development.

Ingram (2013), in his emotionally intelligent social work model (Figure 1.5), combines the historical and ongoing promotion of communication skills in social work practice (for example, the use of many of Roger's techniques of person-centred practice to engage the service user, as discussed in Chapter Three) and the philosophy of emotionally intelligent social work (for example, awareness of our own emotions and those of the service user) as a means to engage service users and enhance outcomes.

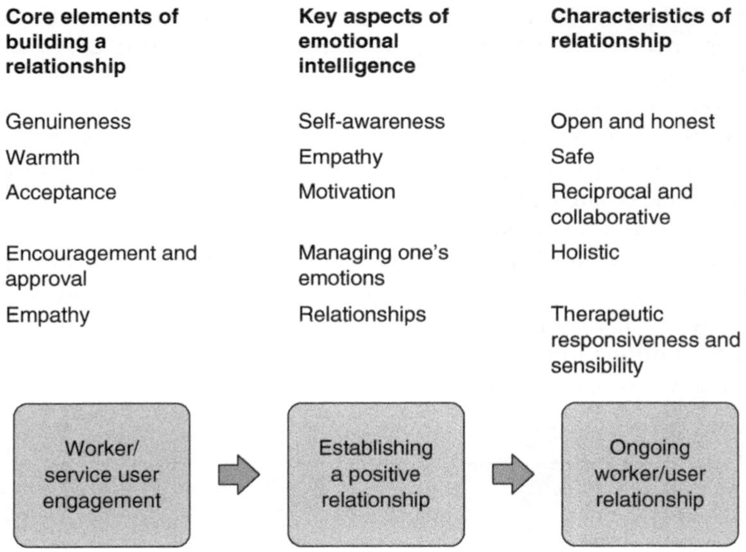

Core elements of building a relationship	Key aspects of emotional intelligence	Characteristics of relationship
Genuineness	Self-awareness	Open and honest
Warmth	Empathy	Safe
Acceptance	Motivation	Reciprocal and collaborative
Encouragement and approval	Managing one's emotions	Holistic
Empathy	Relationships	Therapeutic responsiveness and sensibility

Worker/ service user engagement	⇨	Establishing a positive relationship	⇨	Ongoing worker/user relationship

Figure 1.5 Ingram's (2013) emotionally intelligent social work model.

Ingram (2013) argues that emotional intelligence is both aided by and creates good communication skills, and that both are required to develop good relationships with the service user. Indeed, many of the discussions that will be had throughout the book combine the need for use of *self* and *empathy* (see, in particular, Chapter Five) in your communication, so clearly an understanding and awareness of your emotional intelligence will be highly beneficial to your communication skills' development.

REFLECTIVE TASK 1.3

Reflect back to a time when you had an argument with a loved one. How did your feelings impact on your ability to communicate your feelings and perspective to them?

It is likely that you may have been upset, but responded angrily, said something you did not mean to, or gone quiet to avoid doing just that. But most likely, you did not exhibit your best communication skills. In order to be an emotionally intelligent communicator, you will need to be aware of the impact of your emotions on your ability to communicate. If you are anxious going into the home of a service user who is known to be aggressive, how does this affect your ability to communicate? In Chapter Five, we discuss empathic responses to service user's defensive behaviours (Trevithick, 2011), but it worth remembering here that we too may have conscious or unconscious defensive behaviours, in anticipation of, or in response to difficult situations.

Howe (2008) reminds us that our emotional state will impact on the service user's emotional state; if we are agitated, they are less likely to feel calm. By being aware of this, you can allow for it and plan. Think back to using Gibbs' cycle of reflection – you have just gone through the evaluation and analysis stages within this scenario, so what action plan would you put in place as a coping strategy to resolve and counter your defensive behaviours? As we mentioned in the Introduction, throughout this book you will be asked to think about your communication skills audit. An awareness of your *self* will be critical in this, and an awareness of your emotional wellbeing adds to your emotional intelligence. Of course, if you are calm or happy, the service user will equally respond to a positive mood.

REFLECTIVE TASK 1.4

You go to your general practitioner (GP) with a personal health issue that you are anxious about sharing with them. When you enter the doctor's surgery, they are short tempered when asking you how you are today. When you tell them, they seem judgemental and tell you curtly to take the prescribed medication, and then dismiss you.
    How do you feel after this appointment?

It is possible that you may be reluctant to share the information that you want to, and may be brief in your description, or anxious so forget an important detail? It is likely that you will leave feeling unvalued and 'processed'.

REFLECTIVE TASK 1.4 CONTINUED

When you enter the doctor's surgery, they are interested in you, respond with patience, empathy and understanding at how the personal health issue is affecting you. They talk to you about how you would like to resolve the problem by giving you options.
    How do you feel after this appointment?

It is likely that after the appointment with this doctor you felt valued, that you had been afforded time to explore the issues, and that you had been heard. Imagine, then, that you are a service user, and the difference in your openness to sharing information with a social worker who is accessible and empathic. That is, your emotional intelligence can and will form the basis of an engaging social work relationship.

Hennessey (2011) discusses *relationship-based social work* and argues that relationships are central to our wellbeing, that people are by nature *relationship seekers*. He therefore argues that it is only natural to assume that the quality of the social worker's relationship with the service user will influence the quality of service user engagement, and impact on the success of the outcome. He concludes that in order to use your *self* most effectively within a positive working relationship with a service user, you must be aware of your strengths, moods and areas to develop, and how they will impact on the service user, which is, of course, being emotionally intelligent. However, he reminds us that it is never that simple, as personal and procedural issues will influence your ability to be your natural self. Munford and Sanders (2016) reinforce this perspective in their research into positive outcomes for young people. They found that relationship-based social work utilising empowering and respectful communications enhanced engagement. Chapter Eight on barriers to communication discusses the issues that could impact on your attempt to communicate to the best of your ability and therefore your positive working relationship. Frost et al. (2015) encourage enhancing your practice and development of quality relationship-based social work practice through reflection on the impact of your communication skills on the service user and service provision.

But you will also need to be aware of how others are feeling. Chapter Three on listening and Chapter Five on empathy particularly discuss this issue. To be a good communicator, you will need to be aware of the other person's emotional state, and respond to their needs to optimise communication. This is the second half of being an emotionally intelligent student social worker: to be aware of the other person's emotional wellbeing. Howe (2008) argues that it is imperative that, subsequent to awareness and analysis of your own and the service user's emotional states, that your understanding of the service user's feelings is communicated. He concludes that service users want to feel understood, which enables them to develop a working relationship with you. This is, of course, a key social work principle: to value the service user by listening to them and ensuring that they feel heard.

If you can be aware of the impact of your emotional health and issues that affect your communication, and be aware of the service user's emotional wellbeing and other issues that can influence their presentation and communication, then you can adjust your communication to optimise effectiveness. This concept should also be applied to working with peers and other professionals (see Chapter Eleven on inter-professional working).

The need to be emotionally intelligent is embedded in the PCF and the HCPC. Within Domain 1, Professionalism, there is a requirement to be aware of your safety, health and wellbeing, and the impact of *self* on service users. The HCPC (2016b) *Standards of Conduct, Performance and Ethics* demands that as social workers we ensure we are 'fit to practise'. As a student social worker you have a duty to develop your emotional intelligence to ensure that you can act professionally.

REFLECTION DEVELOPS EMOTIONAL INTELLIGENCE AND RESILIENCE

It is suggested that by reflecting on your communication skills, you will become more aware of your strengths and areas to develop, which will make you more aware of the impact that different physical and emotional influences have on your communication, and your ability to adapt your communication to address the issues. Furthermore, as you develop a proficiency to reflect on service users' reactions and communication patterns, you will enhance your capability to empathise and recognise and understand service users' feelings, and thus your competence to respond appropriately, which will result in enriched communication that meets their emotional needs. By developing your communication skills through reflection and audit, you will inevitably develop your emotional intelligence. This view is supported by Grant et al. (2014), as well as previous research referred to in their research, that reflection enhances emotional intelligence. Howe (2008) argues that reflection is the start of emotional intelligence, it is the application of the reflection that makes us emotionally intelligent. We see this as akin to Gibbs' and Kolb's cycles of reflection, that is, to merely reflect is insufficient, you have to apply the learning from the reflection in the next intervention and continue to reflect to be a reflective practitioner and an emotionally intelligent student social worker.

Whilst this book is not written to ask you to develop your ability to deal with stressful social work interventions, a positive by-product of developing your reflectivity and your emotional intelligence will be that you become more emotionally resilient. As you understand your communication skills better, you will also develop your sense of *self* more. As a consequence, you will gain an understanding of the issues that impact on you and cause you stress, so stimulating reflection on coping strategies that will support you to work with greater emotional resilience. Grant and Kinman (2012) identified that emotional intelligence is a predictor for social workers building their emotional resilience. Greer (2016) argued that resilience could be enhanced through greater self-confidence, self-esteem, self-efficacy, a strengths-based perspective, optimism, coping strategies, and having a support network and a willingness to reflect on areas for development, each of which can also be identified with emotional intelligence. Social work is a stressful role, and the development of greater resilience to support you on the hard days ahead of you can only be a good thing.

COMMUNICATION SKILLS AUDIT: REFLECTION SKILLS

ACTIVITY 1.4

Finally, reflect on your strengths and areas for development in relation to reflection itself, and identify two or three action points for you to develop. To give you support, Table 1.2 provides examples of how a student social worker might do this exercise. Use the box below the example to record your strengths, areas for development and action points.

Table 1.2   Communication skills audit: reflection skills

	Strengths in reflection	Areas for development	Action points to improve reflection skills
Domain 2 Values and ethics	*Listen and value service user's wishes and feelings*	*e.g. Expressing my understanding of the service user's wishes and feelings*	*Develop clarification skills* *Summarise service user's wishes and feelings*
Domain 6 Critical reflection	*I am always able to reflect on my negative input into a situation*	*Enhance identifying my positive input into a situation*	*Balance number of positives to negatives in reflection* *Reflect from a strengths perspective*

As this is your first attempt at undertaking a communication skills audit, take time to reflect on what you have read in this chapter and where you feel your skills lie. Now, reflect on which areas you still need to work on, your areas for development, and think about how you will begin to develop them, your action plan. This exercise will be undertaken at the end of each chapter, so you will develop clearer understanding of your learning needs, which if you share with your practice educator, will help you when you are on placement by ensuring it optimises your development.

CONCLUSION

Reflection is not an easy activity for many social work students, but it is a skill that they have to practise like all other social work skills. Ingram (2015) argues that developing good reflection skills takes time and commitment, but taking that time to develop your skills will enhance your emotional intelligence, and therefore your ability to be a better communicator and a better student social worker. We would argue that reflection should not be seen as a 'chore' to be completed for an assessed or formative task, but as a skill that should underpin your practice to ensure that you are consciously competent in your social work and communication.

It can be argued that emotional intelligence is the combination of your intra-personal and interpersonal skills: how you interpret your thoughts and feelings and express them, and how you interpret the other person's verbal and non-verbal communication and respond to them. Through self-awareness and social awareness, the student social worker can adjust and optimise communication to enhance engagement of service users.

FURTHER READING

Gardener, F. (2014) *Being Critically Reflective*. Basingstoke, Hampshire: Palgrave Macmillan.
Grant, L. and Kinman, G. (eds) (2014) *Developing Resilience for Social Work Practice*. London: Palgrave Macmillan.
Ingram, R. (2015) *Understanding Emotions in Social Work*. Maidenhead: Open University Press.

All these books provide excellent insight into their area and further exploration will develop and strengthen your skills of reflection, resilience and emotional intelligence.

INITIAL ENGAGEMENT

Links to Knowledge and Skills Statements

Adults: person-centred practice; direct work with individuals and families; professional ethics and leadership

Children's: relationships and effective direct work; communication; organisational context

INTRODUCTION

This chapter will discuss the importance for student social workers of initial engagement of service users, and the skills required to do this effectively and efficiently. It will explore the service user's perspective within an initial engagement and explore how student social workers can empathise with a service user's recent and historical history to anticipate and plan for different responses. The chapter will continue with practical planning before meeting a service user, and end with discussion of the practical issues that a student social worker needs to consider in the initial engagement with a service user. Mantell (2013) reflects on the importance of positively engaging service users, seeing this relationship as central to the success of any social work intervention. That is, the initial engagement with a service user can influence the effectiveness of your work, thus it is a critical point in your working relationship with a service user.

INITIAL CONTACT

REFLECTIVE TASK 2.1

What do you think you need to do before you meet your service user for the first time?

You will need to consider how you will make the first contact, and where and when you will meet them; you will need to inform yourself in regard to the service user's case by reading their file and contacting existing involved professionals; and you will benefit from consideration of how the service user may feel at your arrival.

The first interaction with a service user that a student social worker will be required to undertake is to make initial contact with them. The nature of the intervention may dictate the nature of the initial contact: if it is a planned appointment, a letter can be sent; if it is a response to an urgent referral, a telephone call will be more appropriate. You will need to reflect on the service user's likelihood of access to certain types of communication.

CASE STUDY 2.1

You receive a referral from a hostel that supports asylum seekers, stating that Mr Olikara, a Syrian asylum seeker, has started to display symptoms of anxiety and depression, and that they would like you to assess his needs and eligibility for services.

- What are the different ways that might you get in touch with Mr Olikara?
- Are there are issues that would impact on your choice of communication?

There are a number of different ways to make the first contact.

Letter: A letter that states clearly and concisely who you are, your role and your agency, with a clear indication of the purpose of your visit, has merit. Healy and Mulholland recommend 'brevity and logical order' in a letter (2012: 51). By clearly stating the date, time and location of the appointment, you will ensure that the service user understands and remembers the arrangement. You will need to be aware of your agency's procedure: Do certain information leaflets need to be sent out with the letter? Do you need to utilise the agency's headed paper and an agreed font and format? However, a letter can appear impersonal, officious and/or removed. It can be difficult to engage a service user with a formal letter, although in a first contact anything less than formal can be misconstrued. Furthermore, you cannot guarantee that the service user receives or reads the letter. You will also need to clarify that you are using a most recent address. Finally, there is a certain amount of delay in writing a letter and sending it out to a service user. If the matter is an urgent one, this is unlikely to be the preferred method of initial communication.

In Mr Olikara's situation, the benefit of a letter is that he can see the date and time in letter form, and keep it for his information. He would be able to take it to his support worker in the hostel and ask for support in terms of preparation for the appointment. If English was not his first language, he could ask the support worker to translate the letter. Consideration should also be given by the student social worker of determining Mr Olikara's first language and literacy skills, and seeking a translation to send to him. On the other hand, if Mr Olikara is inundated with procedural letters from the Home Office, and is suffering from mental health issues, he may choose not to open the letter, due to anxiety, fear or being overwhelmed.

Telephone call: A telephone call ensures that the service user receives the information and provides a more personal initial engagement. It gives the student social worker the opportunity to explain their role, the purpose of the proposed appointment, and to explore how the service user responds to the first visit. However, it can be difficult to receive a 'cold call', particularly from an official: remember to ask if it is a convenient time to talk, and ensure that you are talking to the correct person. Furthermore, remembering the date and time after a verbal discussion may not be easy for a service user, for example, a service user with dementia. By following the discussion with a letter, you can ensure that details have been made clear. You will also have to consider the dilemma of whether to leave a message if the person does not answer the phone, and how this could be a breach of confidentiality if it is a shared number. If you do leave a message, please ensure that you continue to attempt to talk to the service user directly, do not assume that they are able/willing to access their messages.

Until you speak to Mr Olikara, you may not have the information about his fluency of English. So a telephone call might engage him, or may highlight that English is not his first language and that you will need to engage an interpreter for your appointment. In this situation, a discussion with the referrer may be very helpful to establish if a phone call will be an appropriate method of communication.

Electronic communication: In the current climate, communication using email, text and social media is becoming much more normal and accessible. Chapter Nine will deal with this in more detail. However, you will need to reflect on whether these more informal methods of communication are appropriate for an initial contact. Will the service user know who you are? Can you provide sufficient details to ensure that your role and the purpose of the appointment is clear?

Utilising an online translation service can be an excellent way to communicate quickly and Mr Olikara may engage easily with you using this method of communication. However, thought will have to be given whether this is an appropriate first method of communication, and if explanation needs to be offered and permission sought first.

Unannounced visit: Whilst this should be avoided if possible, sometimes it is necessary. Thought should be given by the student social worker as to whether there are any alternative methods of first contacting the service user: telephone call, text, etc. It will be important that you carry and utilise your agency's identification, and quickly and clearly explain who you are and your agency, and the purpose of your visit. It is likely that this exchange will occur on a doorstep and will determine whether you are able to engage the service user. As the chapter progresses we will return to how to engage the service user.

If an unannounced visit was necessary for Mr Olikara, for example, if his mental health deteriorated and the hostel felt that he would be a danger to himself, and you were unable to contact him by phone, then you could discuss with the hostel support worker if they were either able to talk to Mr Olikara in advance of your visit, or accompany you within the initial contact to support him and establishing the relationship.

PREPARE FOR THE INITIAL MEETING

ACTIVITY 2.1

How will you prepare for the initial contact with Mr Olikara to ensure that you are able to engage him?

You never get a second chance to make a first impression. (Source unknown)

It is therefore very, very important that you spend time preparing for the initial contact. As you prepare to visit a service user, you will need to organise the initial contact. Where is the most appropriate and accessible venue: office appointment, home visit, mutually neutral venue? This will depend on the nature of the appointment, and must be assessed and determined with regard to the agency's procedures, the service user's needs, the content to be discussed, and an initial risk assessment. A home visit can provide security from familiarity or create animosity that the service user's home is being violated. An office visit can alienate the service user if they have to wait in an unwelcoming reception area, or it can provide privacy and confidentiality. You should consider what time works best. Booking to see

Mr Olikara at the time that he has to collect his children from school will not engage him. This takes us back to the previous discussion: will you determine a date, time and location, or will you negotiate this with the service user? If you plan to negotiate a mutually convenient time, have a variety of options and utilise a telephone discussion. You will also need to determine if other people need to be present: support worker, interpreter, partner, etc. If you are taking over the case as a new social worker, you will need to co-ordinate with the exiting social worker so that they can introduce you.

By ensuring you have read the referral, and made contact with the referrer and any other agencies involved, you will have gained some information into the service user's needs. Reading any existing case notes will have two benefits, firstly that you will understand a little of the service user's situation, enabling you to enhance your preparatory empathy (see later in this chapter), and secondly, it will avoid the service user having to repeat previously provided information, which can cause frustration. The referral and case file will enable you to undertake an initial risk assessment, which is important when reflecting on whether a lone worker appointment is appropriate. Nevertheless, Mantell (2013) raises a quiet word of caution that the referral and case file contain only one perspective of the service user, and argues that a breadth of opinions at this stage can avoid pre-judiced initial contact.

If you agree to meet at an office or organisational venue, you will need to book a room, and ensure that it has any resources that you will need. For example, if you need internet access to complete an online assessment, ensure the building has open Wi-Fi or computer access. Have you been to the venue before? If not, you will need to consider how you will reach there, and allow sufficient time to travel, including the possibility of getting a little lost. Punctuality at a first appointment can be key to engaging the service user. You also need to ensure that you have sufficient time to complete the appointment. The time you spend with a service user will vary depending on not only the nature of the appointment but also on the service user's individual needs. You have to plan on the side of a lengthier appointment time, as having to rush away from an initial contact will leave a poor impression. A final note on smaller organisational issues is to ensure that your attire will neither offend nor alienate the service user.

Further preparation must include ensuring that you know and understand your remit for the visit. This will include familiarising yourself with any procedural requirements and any forms or assessments that you will need to complete before, during and after the initial contact. Does your agency's procedure require you to give out any standard information on a first contact, that is, confidentiality, access to records or complaints information leaflets?

Grant and Kinman (2014) argue that being well prepared for an intervention will enhance your confidence and your communication skills, hence making your initial contact more likely to be successful. Furthermore, being organised engages a service user and gains their trust.

REFLECTIVE TASK 2.2

It is time to reflect on your skills. We have discussed the importance of preparation before the initial contact, and the impact of the first impression you make.

- Are you an organised person?
- Do you have good time management skills?
- Do you feel confident navigating unfamiliar streets on a home visit?
- What coping strategies do you have in place to support these vital skills?
- Do you need to develop this area?

Discuss your responses with your supervisor and think about time management and organisational coping strategies.

EMPATHIC PREPARATION

Shulman (2012) recommended 'preparatory empathy' before meeting a service user, that is, anticipating the concerns that a service user might have and how they may communicate them. Trevithick (2012: 188) refers to the practical elements the student social worker must consider as a *checklist*, an example of which is shown in Reflective task 2.2 for this case, but argues that a *reflective* approach to preparation can enhance an empathic approach, which will lead to the student social worker appearing *competent and caring*.

ACTIVITY 2.2

- How might Mr Olikara be feeling about your visit?
- How would you feel if you were sent a letter stating that a social worker was visiting next week?
- How do you act when you feel unsure, anxious or scared?

The student social worker will need to consider the service user's personal history and previous interactions with authority establishments. If this is the service user's first experience of interacting with a social worker, how might they perceive the profession? The media portrays the social work profession as incompetent, inert and over-zealous in equal proportions. It is likely that Mr Olikara will be anxious that you plan to remove his children, section him, or that you will report his mental health issues to the Home Office, which will jeopardise his asylum request or hostel accommodation. Fell and Fell (2014) reflect that asylum seekers can have developed a history of distrust and that the student social worker should make the service user feel welcome. They recommend a strengths-based perspective of recognising the resilience that the service user has had to develop to overcome such adversity. Fell and Fell (2014) remind us that whilst the student social worker may have the power in the initial meeting with an asylum seeker, they have to earn the trust and respect of the service user for them to engage with the service.

By contrast, you may encounter a service user with a strong history of intervention with social workers. They may have been looked after as a child or young person. They may have worked with a colleague or predecessor in the past and not found it an empowering experience. This is not to say your predecessor was a poor social worker. But they may have had to make difficult decisions that impacted on the service provision, and the service user could have experienced this as disempowering. Within this discussion, it is the service user's perspective that we are focusing on, as it is their perspective and how they cope with it that will determine their presenting behaviour.

You will also need to take account of the service user's personal experiences. For example, Mr Olikara is a Syrian asylum seeker. It is likely that he has left his belongings and identity behind, that he has travelled under appalling conditions to reach the UK, and that he has experienced oppression through personal and structural barriers. This may have impacted on his emotional resilience to deal with another professional. Yet, he may have experienced kindness and support within the hostel, and have a growing trust of professionals that you will need to nurture. The referrer states that he suffers from mental health problems, which are as yet unassessed, so he may be having panic attacks which impacts on his presentation.

Warrener (2014) looked at the experiences of service provision of service users and social workers in the area of personality disorder and found that often a service user becomes involved with services having experienced trauma, which can impact on their ability to engage with others. She recommends an empathic response to engage service users.

When feeling anxious, service users will react in a variety of ways, including anger, aggression, silence, submissive agreement or avoidance. You may experience a compliant service user who agrees to everything that you propose. Thus you may need to unpick whether that is what they want or what they think you want them to say. You may experience an assertive service user who is able to advocate for themselves and is clear about their needs and/or rights. You may experience a verbally aggressive service user who feels that you will be unable to help them, and so refuses to listen to you. Or the service user may not attend, or attend and say nothing. Whilst it is important to remember your right to a working relationship without aggression, it is important to reflect on why the service user might be acting in this way. Irrespective of the response you will need to engage them through clear explanation, empathic communication, trustworthy engagement, and demonstrate respect by valuing their wishes and feelings.

In summary, as a student social worker you will need to ensure that you reflect with 'preparatory empathy' to consider the multitude of different ways a service user may be feeling and may react to your arrival, and understand and address those issues in a calm manner. Masocha (2015) reflected on how social workers can, sometimes without realising it, signal a power differential by their use of marginalisation language, of isolating asylum seekers as not being 'one of us'. The implication of this research is that the student social worker needs to be welcoming to the service user, rather than compounding their feeling of social isolation and oppression. However, remember that some service users will be delighted and/or relieved to see you. Gridley et al. (2014) undertook research among service users with a disability and their perspective on good social work practice. They concluded that person-centred work where the service user's wishes and feelings were heard and valued is highly appreciated and important. The social worker is seen as the expert in their field and can maximise the support and services they receive.

INITIAL MEETING

Having ensured that you are on time and know the remit and procedure for the meeting, have gathered information from the referrer and any other involved professionals to aid your appointment, and have thought about how the service user might be feeling, it is time for the initial meeting.

> Research has also identified that first meetings have a lasting emotional impact on service users and therefore are a significant stage for engaging service users in processes of help and change towards achieving that elusive state of partnership working. Woodcock Ross (2016: 55)

On arrival, it will support your initial engagement of the service user if you address some basic issues.

How will you address the service user? Mr Olikara, Farid, uncle, sir? It is important that you ask the service user their preferred name within the relationship.

REFLECTIVE TASK 2.3

- How would you feel if a service user asked you to call them Bruiser?
- Would you offer the service user to call you by your nickname?

It is generally agreed that as a professional you offer the service user your known name, and keep nicknames for your personal life. However, the use of a service user's nickname is less clear. On the one hand, it is a person-centred way to engage the service user, but on the other hand it could blur professional boundaries if a personal name is used, particularly when it is associated with aggression, such as Bruiser. If you are unsure, always confer with your supervisor.

Initial greetings? Whilst being aware of different cultural norms of whether a man or woman sits first, it is polite to offer the service user that choice and respect their response. Sitting in a service user's adopted chair, or placing them in a chair against a door when that heightens their anxiety will alienate them and leave them less willing to engage. You also need to think about different cultural greetings. Whilst a hand-shake may be British, the touching of a Muslim man's hand by a White woman can be considered inappropriate.

Phatic conversation. Thompson (2011) reflects on 'phatic', or social conversa-tion, before moving onto discussing the 'business' of the visit. This can include the very British conversation around 'the weather', sport or polite enquiries after health. As the working relationship develops, remembering past personal details engages a service user well, for example, with an older service user, remembering a daughter's wedding and asking how it was shows respect and that you value them. Sadly, a word of caution: sometimes a polite enquiry as to a service user's health or weekend can trigger anxiety or introduce 'business' too quickly, so ensure that you are respon-sive to a service user's reaction.

Note taking. A perennial dilemma that a student social worker faces is whether to take notes during an appointment. By taking notes in your initial contact, you risk not engaging the service user through the lack of eye contact and lose the opportu-nity for observational assessment. However, attention to detail is critical in an initial contact, details such as date of birth, correct spelling of the name and diagnosis can be mis-remembered if not noted contemporarily.

Confidentiality. It will not be unusual to attend an appointment where another person is present, for example, another professional or a family member or a friend. It is critical that confidentiality is maintained within a social work relationship, par-ticularly in the initial contact. It is imperative that you explore with the service user whether this is a relationship within which they are comfortable to discuss personal and possibly confidential or challenging issues. It may be that you have to make an assessment and decision that the discussion is, at least initially, appropriate for the service user only and have to ask the other person to step outside. Whilst this person may be a significant support to the service user, if you need to raise delicate informa-tion with them, it is important that they are afforded the opportunity to make an informed decision about the presence of another person.

Distractions. As a student social worker you will face a variety of distractions when you undertake a home visit, which you will have to negotiate, as we dis-cuss further in the following chapter. On an initial meeting, whilst establishing a working relationship, this may endanger the engagement process. Nicolas (2015) reflects on the impact of a pet's presence, the television being on, multiple visitors or a mobile phone ringing on the student social worker's ability to engage the ser-vice user, and advises clear and authoritative measures to reduce, if not eradicate, the distraction. It is reasonable to use your own assessment of a situation. But it is important that if you find it distracting your appointment, then you will need to address it sensitively.

Refreshments. A final dilemma a student social worker may have to face is whether to accept refreshments. It is embedded in British culture to offer a cup of tea to any visitor, but generous hospitality runs through many cultures. Many local authorities have policies that dictate that we should not receive gifts from service users, but does a cup of tea fall into this category? How about a piece of cake? A plate of curry? To refuse may, again, disengage the service user through discourteous manners, yet you may not feel comfortable accepting. Whilst, as Koprowska (2014) recommends, you can ask colleagues to gauge a local practice, it may be that you have to take each offer on its merits (and your thirst!).

AGREEING A SHARED AGENDA

It is likely that if you have initiated a contact with a service user, you will have an agenda. Initial contacts often have a procedural agenda of assessment of the situation with a view to establishing need for and availability of service provision. It will not be unusual for the service user to have a different agenda, ranging from your expulsion from their life to you becoming a befriender to support their social isolation. It is critical that you are not only open and honest about your role and agenda, but you must also listen to their agenda, so that a process of negotiation can be undertaken to reach an agreed agenda. Subsequent chapters will discuss listening, clarification, empathy, challenging, etc., the skills that must all be used to achieve a shared understanding of the purpose, nature and process of the social work to follow.

However, in some initial contacts an agreed agenda cannot be negotiated, and time may be needed for both the student social worker and service user to reflect on compromises or consequential actions. Remember that this is the start of a working relationship, and that these take time and care to develop. By utilising your listening skills and valuing the service user's perspective, you may engage them in the longer term.

You will also, at this point, need to set out any agency and procedural expectations. For example, an exploration of the agency's rules about confidentiality will be necessary, including seeking permission from the service user to share information with a third party, such as other agencies or a carer or family member. You will also need to explore the appropriateness of sharing information where the service user may be at risk to themselves or to someone else. You may be required to share how written records will be undertaken and stored, or explain the complaints procedure. Your agency may have a contract that they would require the service user and yourself to complete in regards to expectations of regularity of contact and behaviour. You will need to familiarise yourself with such requirements before an initial visit.

ENGAGING THE SERVICE USER

Lishman (2009) recommends, based on Rogers' (1902–1987) person-centred philosophy, that to build a strong relationship, a student social worker should demonstrate genuineness, warmth, acceptance, encouragement and approval, empathy, and responsiveness and sensitivity. Later chapters will reflect on the importance of Rogers' key tenants of congruence, unconditional positive regard and empathic understanding. Nevertheless, Lishman's list is a clear reminder of the need to place the service user at the centre of initial communications, and that the student social worker's role is that of nurturer, encouraging the service user's ability to share wishes, feelings and perspectives.

This list can be applied with any service user group with whom you will be working. Gridley et al. (2014) found that service users with a disability valued social workers' reliability, making time to spend with them, flexible and knowledgeable responses, and a positive attitude. It is clear that these qualities should be displayed in an initial contact to gain the service user's confidence and engage them effectively. Similarly, Beresford et al. (2008) identify that service users utilising palliative care services value social workers who demonstrate empathy, warmth, respect and listening skills. Ferguson (2016) encourages us to speak to the child or young person, which is as important as speaking to the parent on an initial child protection visit, and that skills of rapport building, patience and *playfulness* are important to engage the child. Ridley et al. (2016) undertook research with a focus on children who are looked after and care leavers, and identified that the young people valued continuity, accessibility and responsiveness, behaviours that all contribute to a committed, relationship-based engagement style.

Irrespective of the service user group, Trevithick (2012) reminds us to utilise our range of skills and knowledge to engage the service user in the optimum way to meet their individual needs. This is absolutely right. You will need to assess the service user's response to your initial communication style and alter it responsively. However, you also need to be 'you'. As you work through this book, you will develop a sense of who you are as a communicator and how to best engage with service users. Do not be afraid to utilise and enhance your personality to demonstrate those critical skills of empathy and warmth and respect, as your natural style will be the most honest, and therefore most engaging. Hennessey (2011) argues that the use of *self* in an intervention is what engages the service user, and that to be a reflective, self-aware student social worker is perhaps more important than the choice of intervention method.

Remember that the service user should be the focus of your initial engagement but that other family members and engaged supporters will also be invaluable in positive interventions. So utilising all the initial engagement skills to engage them will be critical. You will need to reflect on issues of confidentiality when sharing information: what information do they have a right to have? Do you need the service user's permission to share certain information? Recognising their wishes and feelings and considering them along with the service user's wishes and feelings will more likely result in a person-centred and productive outcome. It may be that the family members' or caregiver's views differ from the service user, but without knowledge and reflection on competing needs, they cannot be addressed and resolved.

ENDING YOUR INITIAL CONTACT

When ending your initial contact with a service user, it is helpful to summarise the discussion, utilising the skills discussed later in the clarification and endings chapters (Chapter Four and Chapter Twelve, respectively). It may be helpful to agree on an interim plan, so that you are clear of any tasks that either you or the service user will need to undertake before meeting again. Ensure that you make clear the process from this point, arrange a further appointment if you plan to meet again, and be clear about what the service user can and cannot expect from the agency and yourself. In light of the discussion earlier in the chapter, what is their preferred method of communication, so that you can continue to establish a working relationship? Thompson (2011) recommends concluding with phatic conversation to end less formally.

Remember if you promise to provide information or a service, ensure that you do so, as this will continue to develop the trust and the relationship.

COMMUNICATION SKILLS AUDIT: INITIAL ENGAGEMENT SKILLS

Finally, reflect on your strengths and areas for development in relation to initial engagement and identify two or three action points for you to develop (Table 2.1).

Table 2.1   Communication skills audit: initial engagement skills

	Strengths in initial engagement	**Areas for development**	**Action points to improve initial engagement skills**
Domain 2 Values and Ethics			
Domain 3 Diversity			
Domain 6 Critical reflection and analysis			
Domain 7 Intervention and skills			

CONCLUSION

Your first meeting with a service user, whether it their first interaction with a social worker, or you being introduced into an open case, will be critical to the engagement and success of the working relationship that you will develop. You need to ensure that you are organised and prepared, that your communication is open, and that you are aware of any factors that might influence your, or the service user's, ability to communicate. Develop your own style of communication, but utilise Schön's (1983) reflection in action to identify and respond to the service user's individual need to maximise engagement. Tavormina and Clossey (2017) remind us that much social work intervention is crisis intervention, responding to the service user's presenting need, so remember that, however meticulous your preparation, you will need to be flexible and responsive to the service user's needs.

FURTHER READING

Mantell, A. (ed.) (2013) *Skills for Social Work Practice*. London: Sage. Chapter Six, 'Skills for Engagement', offers an accessible and practical guide to the issues to be considered when first engaging a service user.

Morrison, D. (2016) Being with uncertainty: a reflective account of a personal relationship with an asylum seeker/refugee. *Counselling Psychology Review*, 31(2): 10–21.

CHAPTER THREE

LISTENING

Links to Knowledge and Skills Statements

Adults: role of social workers working with adults; person-centred practice; mental capacity; direct work with individuals and families; professional ethics and leadership

Children's: relationships and effective direct work; communication; adult mental ill health, substance misuse, domestic abuse, physical ill health and disability; abuse and neglect of children; child and family assessment

INTRODUCTION

This chapter will explore the importance of listening and the skills of listening. Research (Forrester et al., 2008) shows that many social workers rely on asking questions, and the chapter will encourage listening and observing. It will explore the skills of silence, non-verbal listening, attending, active listening, minimal encouragers and checking understanding. It will ask you to reflect on the signs that a person is not listening and to reflect on your own skills. The chapter will conclude with a reflection on social work communication skills needed when a service user's limited communication or coherence impacts on your ability to listen, for example if a service user has misused alcohol, their impairment impacts on their communication skills, or when English is not their first language.

PERSON-CENTRED LISTENING

> Active listening skills are complex, but they are the fundamental bedrock of good practice. (Moss, 2015: 13)

As discussed in the Introduction, you will need to determine your professional identity and style of communication. You must also develop a range of communication skills (or a communication skills tool-belt) to ensure that you engage to the best of your ability, given the individual service user's needs. Rogers et al. (2016) reflect that person-centred communication is one that is reactive to the service user's communication needs. Thus by listening to the service user's needs you can assess the best way to communicate and therefore engage with them.

Carl Rogers (1967) introduced the concept of *client-centred therapy*, which has been adapted within social work and forms the backbone of person-centred working. He reflected that the quality of the worker was important as a predictor of a successful outcome. A student social worker will be considered *genuine* if they show clear listening skills, and their non-verbal and verbal communications are *congruent* (in agreement) with each other. When listening to the service user's perspective, we must not make judgements about their wishes and feelings. Instead we should offer a positive response to them, to ensure that they feel respected and valued – in other words, offer *unconditional positive regard*.

Gathering a service user's wishes and feelings is enshrined in legislation: from the Children Act 1989, which states that both parents' and a child/young person's wishes and feelings should be heard and balanced against risk, to the Mental Capacity Act 2005, where even when a person is assessed as not to have capacity to make a decision, that his or her views must always be sought and considered by the decision maker. Person-centred planning was entrenched in *Valuing People* (Department of Health, 2001) and *Valuing People Now* (Department of Health, 2010), and embedded into practice with service users with a learning difficulty through *Putting People First* (HM, Government, 2007). This meant that the wishes and feelings of service users with a learning difficulty had to be sought, heard and responded to. Listening to service users' views has become an everyday task for social workers, and that necessitates student social workers to develop their listening skills. Most recently, the Care Act 2014 gives the local authority the duty to undertake a person-centred assessment, that is assessing service users' needs with them so that their perspective is recognised and respected.

Partnership is a commonly used term within social work to imply that a social worker is seeking the wishes and feelings of a service user, and that they will be involved in the decision-making process about matters that will impact on them. The principle is that if you *empower* a service user to make a decision with you, they will be more able to make it without support next time. Also, they will have ownership of the decision, so they are more likely to engage with the process. By undertaking active person-centred listening, you will be able to work in partnership much more effectively.

NON-JUDGEMENTAL LISTENING

As a student social worker, it is imperative that you act in a non-judgemental manner, and this also applies when you are listening. It is not uncommon to approach a professional discussion with an agenda, an outcome that we would like or a direction to be taken, be it a procedural agenda, or based on a professional value base. The student social worker will be aware of the need to act in a certain way, deliver an agreed outcome or meet a deadline. It is important when listening that we put this aside. The service user's views are worthy of being heard, without assuming that they will say a certain thing or hold a particular perspective. In the listening stage, the student social worker is gathering the service user's views. The analysis will come later: the ethical dilemma of balancing a mum's needs to be with her child, with the child's need to be protected from risk of significant harm, the procedural model to follow, and the lack of resources to undertake good practice. At this moment in time, the service user should be heard, and that can only happen by non-judgemental listening.

CASE STUDY 3.1

The student social worker receives a referral to a domestic abuse incident, where a young child, Molly, is present. On making enquiries, other issues are raised, so the student social worker agrees with her manager that an initial assessment should be undertaken.

The student social worker goes to the house with a colleague and expects to hear from the partner Harriet, that she is abused or 'walked into the door'. Instead, she hears that both Harriet and her partner have a mild learning difficulty and experience hate crime from the neighbours, which can lead to her partner expressing his frustration in verbal aggression. He expresses a strong desire to resolve both the hate crime and his reaction.

The student social worker is able to discuss the hate crime with housing, access an appropriate anger management course, and call an adult safeguarding meeting to support the family, rather than view this as a child protection issue.

If the student social worker had assumed that she knew the outcome in respect to the domestic violence issue, or had a judgemental perspective on the parent's ability to parent effectively, she would not have been able to develop a person-centred and appropriate support plan. Williams and Evans (2013) argue that a commonly held view by social workers is that parents with learning difficulties are not able to parent well enough or appropriately to meet their child's needs. This is supported by a survey in 2005 by the NHS, which found that 7% of people with a learning difficulty had a child, and that 50% of those parents had had their child removed.

Tarleton (2015) recommends 'parenting with support'. She reflects that parents with a learning difficulty may need long-term support to enable them to parent to the best of their ability. In the plan in Case study 3.1, the student social worker was able to identify the issues to support safe parenting.

NON-VERBAL COMMUNICATION

Your personal mannerisms can convey a lack of interest. For example, a student social worker played with her hair throughout an assessment. It was a sign of anxiety, but to the service user it said that she was more interested in her appearance than in them.

REFLECTIVE TASK 3.1

Do you have any personal habits that may indicate a lack of attention? You may need to ask a loved one to kindly to share their observation. We often have unconscious habits that can say the wrong thing to the service user that we need to be aware of and adapt.

How can you try to be more self-aware of your non-verbal communication?

Non-verbal communication is our physical response to a situation. It includes facial expressions, physical gestures, tone of voice and eye contact. Non-verbal communication informs how we interpret verbal communication. We take in far more than what is said. Some of that will be very conscious observations: a nod of the head or a visible pull away from a spider. However, much of the non-verbal listening that we do will be unconscious observation of people. Our eyes and brains observe reactions to questions or statements that words do not express.

ACTIVITY 3.1

In a small group, appoint a leader. The leader will stand in the middle and demonstrate and give instructions for the rest to follow, for example pat your head. The leader will continue to give simple instructions, but part way through they will say one instruction and demonstrate another. How does the group respond?

Discuss with the group how confusing it felt when the verbal and non-verbal directions differed.

A skilled social worker will listen to a service user's body language as well as the spoken conversation. Gast and Bailey (2014) discuss 'communication cues', whereby an active observer within a conversation can hear reactions and perspectives from the observed person's non-verbal responses and body language. Gast and Bailey reflect that a person's eyes, facial expression and body language indicate feelings, thoughts and responses.

Attention must also be given by student social workers to cultural differences in non-verbal communication norms. Different cultures may value different responses to similar situations. A common example is the difference in interpretation of finishing all the food on your plate: in Britain, it is a compliment to the chef, but in Japan it can be insulting as it means the serving was insufficient. Whilst a student social worker is unlikely to be in a position where they will be eating a meal in Japan, it is an easily identifiable example. Similarly, a Muslim man refusing to shake the hand of a young female White British non-Muslim student social worker is not an insult, but an indication that his faith does not allow him to touch people of a different gender.

ACTIVE LISTENING

ACTIVITY 3.2

Think of a time you weren't listened to: while shopping, by a doctor or a family member.

- Think about the conversation, what demonstrated to you that you were not being listened to?
- Were they checking their watch, not responding to your perspective, or just appeared 'glazed over'?
- What impact did this have on you?

Firstly, think about how you felt. You may have felt devalued, angry or upset, it may have resulted in you being less invested in that conversation and less keen to be with them. Did you feel that you would not go back to that shop again? If our service users feel that you have not listened, imagine how they will feel. It is likely that they will be frustrated or angry with you, and will be much less likely to want to work with you to resolve any issues.

Service users will instinctively read *your* non-verbal communication. This means that if you are not interested or distracted, they will read your lack of attentive, or active, listening and not feel valued, and be less likely to share their wishes, feelings, opinions and history, which may result in significantly inappropriate decisions being made.

Ask a friend if they will tell you about a recent happy event, for example, a night out, family meal, football match win, etc. Half a minute into their story, stop listening, and make it obvious. How does your friend react?

Did your friend notice? Did they continue to tell their story, or did it fizzle out when you were not interested? Think of the impact a lack of interest will have on a service user when they are unsure whether to share details of their life with you. Do you think that you would be likely to gain more or less information if they think that you feel they are not worth listening to?

Egan (2014) recommends that in order to demonstrate your active listening, you should practise talking to service users utilising the SOLER system:

Square, or straight, position facing the interviewee: By positioning yourself so that you are facing the service user, you are able to convey with your non-verbal behaviour that you are interested and giving them your attention. But be aware there is a fine line between interested and intimidating. When you think about the power issues discussed above, you will need to ensure that this is appropriately undertaken, utilising the rest of SOLER to support this.

Open position: Again, think about how the service user will read your non-verbal communication in regard to your body language. Traditionally, arms crossed tightly indicates a defensive or uninterested person, whilst slouching can indicate the social worker may be so laid back that they will not undertake the agreed intervention. Whilst one can argue about this (particularly on a cold day!), practise a relaxed but open sitting position.

Lean towards the service user when appropriate: Leaning in to a service user can convey empathy or particular interest, when accompanied with a matching tone of voice. However, it can also convey power, that you feel that the service user must do as you say. Clearly, this position should be used at the appropriate time, not throughout a conversation.

Eye contact: In White British communication, it is customary to provide a significant level of eye contact to show the other person that you are listening and engaged. Whilst you must remember that other cultures do not always follow the same philosophy, it will be helpful to practise your eye contact if you find this difficult.

Relaxed communication: In order to support each of the earlier points of SOLER, you will need to be relaxed in your speech and your demeanour, for example, not fiddling with your watch or hair. This will give the service user confidence that you are capable and confident, which will engage them further.

Clearly, you will need to practise each of these, and some will be easier for you than others. They will need to be practised with a congruent tone of voice, so that the service user knows that you are being natural. It will feel unnatural at first, and you may have to concentrate on it. Of course, the problem can be that you are so busy trying to make sure that you are listening, that you are distracted by your concentration on it! Practise utilising SOLER in conversation with family or friends, where you can feel safe that you might miss some information when you are concentrating on your body position.

> Listening attentively conveys interest and respect. (Koprowska, 2014: 79)

Other ways to demonstrate that you are listening is to nod your head or use quiet noises of agreement, for example, 'mmm', 'yeah', etc. These are essential ways to show a service user that you are part of the conversation whilst you are listening. By paraphrasing and summarising the content of their discussion, you will be able to show that you were listening, as you have heard and (hopefully) understood the content. This will be discussed further in Chapter Four on clarification.

Dunhill (2010) discusses the importance of active listening, in particular ensuring that your listening is appropriate to the service user group, for example, that it is age appropriate. They recommend engaging young people through young people's preferred communication style. In today's age, it may be that text discussions or using social media (with privacy settings) makes a young person's wishes and feelings more accessible and immediate. Dunhill (2010) reflect that to communicate well with young people and children, the student social worker must develop a *good rapport* with them, by valuing them and showing them respect, which can be done by listening to the service user.

RESPONSIVE LISTENING

So then, you are listening to the service user's verbal and non-verbal communication, and they are responding to your verbal and non-verbal attentive listening. Now you need to balance listening, whilst ensuring that you are still participating in the conversation: you cannot just listen. Conversation is like a game of table-tennis, you need to hit the ball back to keep the volley going. Whilst you must listen to the service user, you must also utilise open questions to continue to stimulate the discussion. You will need to provide feedback to the service user to show that you have been listening, show empathy, clarify that you have understood correctly, and ask the service user to listen to their own perspective back to provoke reflection. These issues will be covered in subsequent chapters, but it is important to recognise that listening is but one element of a successful social work dialogue.

Part of listening is also about analysing and adjusting your responses to the service user to maximise engagement. Thompson calls this *feedback*, where he describes 'receiving information from them and adjusting one's own contribution to the conversation accordingly' (2011: 90–1). Whilst listening to the factual content of the conversation, one should also be listening to the verbal and non-verbal responses that inform you if the service user is happy, anxious, angry or frustrated. This will enable you to further the conversation in the most productive manner. If you relate this back to your emotional intelligence (discussed in Chapter One), you will see that responsive listening requires an emotionally intelligent response: you will be required to understand the barriers to your listening (see Chapter Eight) and adapt to address them; you will be required to understand how a service user is feeling, and show empathic responses that demonstrate that you have heard and understood their perspective. In short, you will need 'to have a high degree of self-awareness and be attuned to the thoughts, feelings and responses of others' (Rogers et al., 2016: 23).

CASE STUDY 3.2

The hospital social worker visits an older gentleman, Mr Cook, shortly before discharge from the ward, to undertake the pre-discharge assessment. She asks him what he wants on discharge, and he begins a long monologue on his preferred discharge. The social worker, however, is not listening. She has already determined that he will be discharged home and will be supported by his son who lives locally. She feels she has no relevant role and is mentally planning her next appointment.

However, as a consequence, Mr Cook begins to feel that she does not value his wishes and feelings and becomes angry with her. He is scared about being isolated, and has expressed a desire to be active once he returns home, but the social worker was not listening to him.

- How could she have listened more productively?
- How could she have used *feedback* to make the assessment more effective?

It is clear that the social worker should have been focused on the service user. Tanner et al. (2015) reflect on the need for *user-centred transitions* for older people facing admissions and discharges from hospitals and care establishments. They argue that the older person is likely to have better physical and emotional outcomes if they have been listened to when determining the care plan. They recognise that the element of *control* in the decision-making process enables them to be more engaged in the process and to feel empowered, and thus happier.

It is important to *hear* what is said, this can be achieved by some simple listening skills. Always wait until the other person has finished speaking – do not try to finish their sentences as this will put them off expressing their wishes and feelings. This values the service user and their opinions, and will elicit engagement and information. Koprowska (2014) recommends the avoidance of repetitive questions, as it implies that you have not listened to the service user's response and disengages them. She also highlights the essential skill of utilising silence to let the service user think.

Horwath and Tarr (2015) undertook research that looked at children at risk of significant harm from neglect within child protection cases. They remind us that listening to a child's wishes and feelings can be done through observation as well as spoken word, and also that a child's wishes and feelings should be considered with all other facts in context of an assessment of risk. They argue that hearing the child's perspective of their experience should inform the social worker's assessment, as children's resilience and vulnerability differs from child to child.

CASE STUDY 3.3

Isabelle is a 15-year-old young woman who presents at the duty office demanding that she is taken 'into care'. She is angry and demands that she gets what she wants.

You are the duty social worker, and ask her about the issues. You have two choices: you can tell her that she needs to calm down and that she will not be able to be accommodated as that is not the local authority policy; or you can listen to her concerns and explore with her the issues that have led her to wish to be accommodated, whilst knowing that it is not an option, as it is against the local authority policy. Which approach will be more productive?

On the one hand, telling Isabelle that her behaviour is not acceptable may be deemed to be appropriate within the council's respect to staff policy and an open and honest approach towards the policy of not accommodating will certainly help her to make an informed decision. On the other hand, however, it is rare that a service user is angry without antecedents. Chapter Two on initial engagements reflects on Shulman's (2016) preparatory empathy and reminds us to reflect on the reason behind a service user's challenging behaviour. By listening to Isabelle's perspective, it is hoped that you will engage her into an exploration of what has led to her demand, and be able to support her to identify realistic areas that can be addressed with your support.

CASE STUDY 3.3 CONTINUED

Isabelle tells you about how her relationship with her mum has deteriorated since she has had a new partner, and her feelings of rejection, loss and isolation. You are able to engage her with a local youth group and arrange mediation between mum and daughter that leads to a happier relationship for both women.

CHALLENGES TO LISTENING

Sometimes a service user lacks communication clarity, perhaps because of drug or alcohol misuse, mental health or language difficulties. That is, they are difficult to listen to because of a factor impacting on their verbal communication. It can be a sign of stress when a service user becomes less coherent in a conversation, or it can run through the whole conversation. The student social worker will need to support and encourage the service user and have patience to enable them to say what they need to. Listening becomes even more important, because gathering their wishes and feelings when self-advocacy is difficult will be critical in the decision-making process.

It is as much about our ability to hear what is being said as the service user's communication impairment. For example, Williams and Evans (2013) remind us of the 'mutuality' of a service user's disability when working with a service user with a learning difficulty, for example Harriet in Case study 3.1. The social model of disability is based on society's response to a person's impairment, their ability to respond appropriately (Oliver, 1983). Therefore, when communicating with a service user with a learning difficulty or disability, it is our duty to ensure that their communication is heard and understood. Many service users with a disability will be able to communicate well, and assumptions should not be made that they will not be able to do so. However, when working with a service user with a disability whose communication is limited, the student social worker must first understand their preferred method of communication and then work within it. For many service users with a learning disability, it is important to ask single topic questions, so that they can respond to each issue individually. Furthermore, it is important to allow time for the service user to express their wishes and feelings, and not to assume responses.

Other times when listening may be difficult for you can be when the service user has a strong regional accent or when English is not their first language. Firstly, time must be spent allowing yourself to acclimatise to the accent. You will have to strike a fine balance between asking for clarification to ensure that you have heard appropriately and also respecting the service user's communication. There is nothing more frustrating for both of you than having to keep repeating yourself!

REFLECTIVE TASK 3.2

How would you ensure that you understand what was said if you were struggling to understand an asylum seeker's explanation of their journey here?
   Reflect on how you would feel.
   Reflect on how they might feel.

You might feel awkward or self-conscious that you have to ask them to repeat phrases, or be tempted to *guess* what they meant, or jump in to help them, assuming what they are going to say. Each of these will inhibit your ability to hear what they need to say. Or the service user may feel embarrassed, frustrated or reluctant to continue as you work with them to understand what they wish to say. This may restrict their ability to convey their wishes and feelings, and so your ability to gather their wishes and feelings. Reflecting on the discussion in Chapter One about emotional intelligence, you will need to be aware of both your own and their emotions to ensure that the communication is not sabotaged.

Using a translation service to listen to a service user's wishes and feelings can be both effective and full of peril. Sawrikar (2013) researched the use of a translator in child protection services in Australia, and concluded that only about 15% of the translated discussion accurately expressed the family's wishes and feelings. Whilst acknowledging other issues (including the impact of quality and availability of the translation service) she noted that the social worker's skills and time impacted significantly on the successful use of a translation service. Maiter et al. (2017) concur that investing in training and understanding of the utilisation of positive translation services enhances communication. Whilst an interpreter can effectively translate a service user's perspective, the student social worker's ability to interpret non-verbal communication can be diminished. Furthermore, you will have to practise looking at the service user rather than the interpreter to listen effectively.

ACTIVITY 3.4

In a group of three, ask person A to tell person B something. Ask person B to tell person C what person A just said. Person C needs to look at person A throughout the discussion.

- How does this feel? Is it odd to disregard the person who is speaking to you?
- Do each of you feel that person B successfully repeated what person A had said? Reflect on the importance of nuances of speech when utilising an interpreter.

There is both merit in and dangers of using a family member or friend to interpret your discussion. Of course, instant access to a translator can be invaluable, and the service user will have an established relationship with them, which can be comforting in a stressful situation and can reduce anxiety. However, it can also raise issues of confidentiality: without a neutral translator, we cannot ensure consent or neutrality; we may be unaware of the translator's own agenda or relationship to the service user. We may, inadvertently, place the service user at risk by talking to an inappropriate family member or friend. But irrespective of the issues discussed here, the use of an interpreter is always beneficial to the service user: it is up to you as the social worker to be aware of the potential pitfalls and facilitate a successful translated communication.

A further challenge to the student social worker's ability to listen can occur when working with a service user who is less coherent due to mental health or substance misuse. For example, the student social worker must first assess the ethical appropriateness of the timing of the communication. Is this a discussion that can be put back to another time when the service user will be able to express themselves more coherently or have greater capacity? If it is a discussion that needs to happen, you need to bear in mind that you may receive a dis-inhibited response, or that the service user may talk more quickly or slowly, and listening may need more concentration. You will also need to ensure that they have understood your perspective and consider leaving a note to summarise the discussion.

It must be noted that sometimes the service user's perspective of whether they have been listened to can be different from that of the student social worker. McLeod (2006) undertook research with young people in care and found that whilst the social worker felt that they had listened well and recorded their wishes and feelings, the young person did not feel listened to unless they received the requested service. It will always be important to explain that you hear the service user, although that does not guarantee that their requested services will be viable. Managing expectations is an ethical dilemma that student social workers sometimes face. Certainly, a Care Act 2014 assessment requires the service user's wishes and feelings and needs to be listened to and respected, yet these are carried out within a resource budget, allocations criteria and service availability climate.

COMMUNICATION SKILLS AUDIT: LISTENING SKILLS

Finally, reflect on your strengths and areas for development in relation to your listening skills and identify two or three action points for you to develop (Table 3.1).

Table 3.1   Communication skills audit: listening skills

	Strengths in listening	Areas for development	Action points to improve listening skills
Domain 1 Professionalism			
Domain 2 Values and ethics			
Domain 6 Critical reflection and analysis			
Domain 7 Intervention and skills			

CONCLUSION

Listening to the person to whom you are talking is critical in communication: you have to hear the service user's perspective in order to gather their wishes and feelings, to assess the situation, or to offer support. Non-judgemental listening, where you *hear* what is said without a subjective perspective, will enable you to engage the service user effectively. And remember that your non-verbal listening needs to be as good as your verbal listening: to show that you actually are listening. Rogers et al. (2016) remind us that you will need to use all your communication skills to listen effectively: your initial engagement will enable you to listen, your clarification and empathy skills to actively listen to the service user's perspective, and your challenging skills to determine real wishes and feelings.

FURTHER READING

Koprowska, J. (2014) *Communication and Interpersonal Skills in Social Work*. London: Sage. Chapter Five has a useful analysis of the importance of listening and the skills of listening.

Rogers, M., Whitaker, D., Edmondson, D. and Peach, D. (2016) *Developing Skills for Social Work Practice*. London: Sage. Chapter Two, 'Active listening skills', offers advice and practical tips on listening skills.

CLARIFICATION

Links to Knowledge and Skills Statements

Adults: person-centred practice; effective assessments and outcome-based support planning; professional ethics and leadership

Children's: relationships and effective direct work; communication; adult mental ill health, substance misuse, domestic abuse, physical ill health and disability

INTRODUCTION

This chapter will consider the importance of clarifying details and information relayed by service users and professionals to ensure that misunderstandings do not occur. It will discuss how to use open versus closed questions, paraphrasing, mirroring and summarising. It will ask the reader to reflect on the incongruence of verbal and non-verbal communication, and how to clarify meaning with a service user.

The chapter will also reflect on ensuring that as a communicator you achieve clarity of information for those with whom you communicate. It will consider the importance of ensuring that a service user hears what they have said as a therapeutic tool, and that clarification supports the service user to identify and address the issues with which they are faced. By ensuring you have heard and understood the service user's wishes and feelings you will be able to work in a person-centred way.

THE IMPORTANCE OF UNDERSTANDING CORRECTLY

ACTIVITY 4.1

Think of a time when you and a friend or family member 'got hold of the wrong end of the stick', and 'got your wires crossed'.

- Perhaps you tried to meet them on the wrong day, time or location?
- How did the misunderstanding impact on your ability to meet efficiently?
- When you talked about it, was there a sense from each of you of feeling you were in the right or of guilt?
- How did you move forward from here?

It is likely that you have experienced times which have resulted in an argument, or at least discussion, as you both express your frustration or even anger, at the situation. Hopefully you were able to explain your perspective and listen to the other person's perspective and the matter was resolved. However, you may both have 'stewed' on that frustration and it impacted on your view of that person. Leaving a service user frustrated or angry is not a positive way to engage them, even if it can later be resolved by talking through it. Clarification is a preventative approach to ensure that all have a shared understanding of the discussion.

It is important when discussing something that you clarify the agreed outcome. In order to ensure that both (or all) parties have heard and processed the same information, and come to the same conclusion of the discussion, a simple summary of the outcome can avoid misunderstanding and confusion. Without clarity and agreement, a simple appointment can lead to anxiety, anger or frustration. Put into social work terms: additional work will be needed on top of a busy caseload to resolve a minor mistake that could disengage a service user. Much of the time you will be required to advocate for a service user, but how can you do that if you do not understand what they want? If you establish a support plan to meet their needs, but are meeting the wrong needs this will be very counterproductive and disengage the service user.

WHY DO WE NEED TO CLARIFY WITHIN A DISCUSSION?

When we are in a discussion with a service user, colleague or other professional, we will, as discussed in previous chapters, have an agenda. This can be procedural, personal or professional. As a student social worker, you will work hard to address any bias from a personal perspective, and will approach the discussion non-judgementally. You will also work to address 'distractions' (discussed in Chapter Eight), to ensure active listening. However, no matter how hard you work to minimise misunderstandings, they still occur. This is because when we hear information, we process it utilising a variety of filters. This will include your professional values, your interpretation of the service user's verbal and non-verbal communication, your previous experiences and interests, including your cultural, gender, age and class experiences, and your knowledge of the service user.

REFLECTIVE TASK 4.1

As a group, take time to have a beverage in the local coffee shop. Now, each identify one main observation about the experience, then share and compare these factors.

How do these vary? Do different people have different priorities, perspectives and observations?

One of you may focus on the quality of the coffee, another the décor of the coffee shop, a third the mannerisms of the waiter/ress. All are valid perspectives. Perhaps one of you has been a waitress and felt for them with a difficult customer, or another had already had a coffee, so felt resistant to being there? What about the direction you were each facing, or if you were sitting on different styles of chair? The reality is that we all interpret situations through our individually constructed filters. Further to this is the importance of an understanding of the social construction of how society views social work intervention and how this impacts on our values which inform intervention choices both individually and procedurally. For example, when tragedies such as Victoria Climbié's and Baby P's deaths triggered public outcry and social work practice review, the generic social work response was a move towards a more risk-averse culture, which was contradicted with budget cuts within times of austerity that reduced the preventative social work provision available within many areas. Llewellyn et al. (2015) reflect on the idea that some children are seen as more deserving of protection than others by society, for example asylum seekers. They also reflect that some service user groups are seen by society as more deserving of support than others, which impact on social work assessment. For example, in Case study 4.1, should a mother who 'does not leave her partner' deserve the support of a social worker if they will not 'help themselves'? Or should the student social worker be exploring the social barriers to understand the reason behind her seemingly short sighted choice, such as the stigma of becoming a single mother dependent on benefits, or having a faith that denies marriage breakdown? These are value-laden questions that you will need to reflect on to ensure that you understand why service users make the decisions they make, and why the service provision response made is the appropriate one.

Social cognitive processes mean that we are influenced subconsciously by our previous experiences and societal influences, which can result in a difference between what the service user says and what the student social worker hears, a cognitive distortion or bias. In social work, it is important that we do not put our thoughts and feelings into interpreting the service user's perspective, which we call *transference* and was first proposed by Freud in 1923. In order to avoid cognitive bias it is critical that we 'check if we have got the right idea': clarify that we understand the service user's perspective. If we misunderstand what the service user is trying to say, we cannot respect their wishes and feelings, cannot provide a service that meets their need, cannot advocate for them appropriately. In order to work utilising relationship-based social work, as discussed in the Introduction, we need to clarify that we have heard and understood correctly. It is *your* responsibility to ensure that you have heard and understood the service user's perspective, and therefore clarification is a critical skill in your social work communication skills repertoire. Trevithick (2012) argues that clarifying questions enable the student social worker to make informed decisions, by ensuring that they represent the service user appropriately and present the facts accurately. In addition, as O'Brien (2016) notes, using our perspective to *reframe* rather than misinterpret can be a useful tool to challenge the service user to consider their situation from a different, perhaps more positive, perspective.

CASE STUDY 4.1

You have been working with Clara for four months, since your placement began. She has suffered from domestic abuse and her two children are on the Child Protection Register. This morning you have received a referral from the police stating that there was a new incident of domestic abuse last night, and have gone to visit Clara to clarify the situation.

- When you visit Clara, you listen to her story, but some details are unclear and seem confused. What skills will you use to ensure that you have a clear picture of events?
- Are there any value perspectives or personal experiences that might impact on your cognitive bias?

It is normal in child protection social work to clarify the information from a referrer where possible. You might contact the police officer involved for a verbal update, as a written referral may not provide the detail or inference that a conversation might do so. You could also contact the children's school to see if they have noticed anything that morning that would indicate a change in the children's presentation. By doing this, you will be attending the appointment with information to enable you to make an informed decision.

When discussing with Clara, you will need think about how you will clarify the information that she gives you. Remember: she is a victim of domestic abuse and will need to be afforded empathy and support. But also remember: the children have been placed at risk, and you need to clarify information to be able to make informed decision about their safety. As with all social work communication, an open and honest approach with the service user will elicit engagement. By reflecting on your confusion over Clara's recount, you can work through the incident together to explore what happened.

POWER WITHIN SOCIAL WORK COMMUNICATION

Whilst you may feel powerless as a social work student on placement, it is fair to say that your service user is likely to feel significantly less powerful than you. You hold the ability to make life-changing decisions, which may make a service user feel at your mercy. It is therefore vital that you address this perceived and real power imbalance by working in partnership using person-centred communication. Utilise the clarification techniques suggested below to ensure that you have understood the service user's wishes and feelings, but you also have to be open to asking and hearing about what the service user wants.

CASE STUDY 4.2

Even within the most serious of child protection cases, irrespective of the long-term outcome of the care plan for the child, the parents deserve to be treated with respect and in an open and honest way.

Reflect for a second on how you would talk to parents where neither one took ownership for serious injuries to an eight-week old baby.

It might be that your instinct is to allow your protective feelings for this badly injured child and personal values to impact on the quality of any communication. However, think how the impact of a hostile attitude, and use of the care proceedings as a power-laden threat, could thwart the social work process. Using a more open dialogue, the parents might be able to share how the child was hurt, which would facilitate a care plan that addressed the risk factors, protected the child and enabled the child to have a safe relationship with their parents.

When undertaking your communication skills audit throughout the book, your aim is to enhance your communication skills to engage the service users to lead to better outcomes. A positive contribution towards this is both the acknowledgement of the power differential and communicating in a way that minimises the power. By listening to the service user, clarifying their perspective, and acting to meet their wishes and feelings you will be able to demonstrate that you wish to work *with* them. Always use your emotional intelligence to reflect on how your communication impacts on the service user: use your power to engage not disengage the service user.

METHODS OF CLARIFICATION

The main methods of clarification are:

- Questions
- Mirroring and paraphrasing
- Summarising

Questions

A variety of question types are available to student social workers: open, closed or leading. One would strongly advocate against utilising a *leading* question, where you provide the service user with the answer for them to confirm, as it will prevent you from hearing the service user's wishes and feelings or perspective. Moreover, it will neither empower the service user to express their own opinion nor show them respect.

Closed questions, those which elicit a yes or no answer, can be helpful to clarify factual information the service user has provided when you are unsure as to the content of the discussion: for example, 'Do you mean that he hit you three times in the face?' Additionally, they can be useful when gathering information or obtaining a clear response to enable an assessment, for example, with Clara you might ask 'Were the children in the house at the time of the fight?' However, closed questions have the risk of sounding judgemental.

A better option may have been an *open* question, 'Where were the children at the time?', which would enable Clara to feel free to respond without direction. *Open* questions start with enquiring words: why, where, when, how, which, who? They ask for a response from the service user's perspective and enable you to gather information and build towards your informed decision making. Often an open question enables the service user to explore the situation. The question 'I have a report of an incident last night Clara, can you tell me what happened?' will enable Clara to reflect on her own factual recollection of the experience of the domestic abuse and share information with you, and also may also enable her to explore her feelings and perspective of the incident.

Trevithick argues that questions that start with *what* are 'immensely adaptable' (2012: 203), as they are perhaps the most open of all questions: 'What did you do when he hit you? She argues that questions that start with *why* can be seen as judgemental, 'Why did you respond in that way when he hit you?', so these need to be asked with caution. Keeling and van Wormer (2012) identify that social work intervention can make a domestic abuse victim feel they are to blame, and it is clear that *why* questions will exacerbate that feeling of responsibility.

It is worth remembering that open and closed questions are both an important part of your communication repertoire, and you will need to develop the skills of using both styles to suit the intervention. For example, you may start an intervention with closed questions and develop open questions as you explore an area further, to gain clarification. As you develop, you will recognise that there is a continuum of open and closed questions, and that you utilise these nuances to gain clarification by engaging the service user in the optimum way to meet their needs.

You will also need to think about *how* you ask questions: the tone of your voice can indicate care and concern or authority and disapproval.

ACTIVITY 4.2

Ask your colleague 'Why did you prioritise taking a lunch break?' in as many different tones of voice as you can. How do they feel depending on the intonation?

You will quickly realise that how you express the same words can significantly impact on how your question is heard and received. Taking a lunch break is a very positive habit, and this question should be a caring, interested one that implies approval. However, it can be laden with accusations of laziness that lead the person to feel guilt or shame. Reflect on how you can ensure that your questions are positive and empower the service user and do not degrade them.

Both Lishman (2009: 24) and Koprowska (2014) warn the student social worker not to *interrogate* the service user with a series of questions, and to think about the impact of their questions. The skill for you as the student social worker to develop is a style of conversation that naturally asks questions and develops the information gathering and assessment so that the service user does not feel inundated by your questions. To clarify information, sometimes you will have to ask the same question in different ways: to ensure that the service user understands what you are asking and the information that you seek. Avoid repetition of the same phrase, and reflect on how you can approach the issue from a different angle, or come back to it later in the discussion. But reflect on other chapters too: Koprowska's (2014) perspective not to repeat questions should be borne in mind, even if the purpose is to clarify information and the question has been asked in different ways. There comes a point when you will have to accept that you cannot elicit this information today. Keeling and van Wormer (2012) recognise that when working with victims of domestic abuse, the procedural model of information gathering to inform decision making can be an oppressive one, designed to protect the child at the expense of the protection of the mother. They recommend an empowering model of information gathering that recognises the mother's strengths and understanding of her own situation and needs, as a powerful intervention to resolve the issue positively.

Jenney et al. (2014) argue that women who suffer domestic abuse have become expert in protecting their child/ren, and that a student social worker should listen to their perspective to clarify how they can work together to further develop the family's coping strategies to best meet the family's needs by using a strengths-based perspective. Furthermore, they suggest that a child protection plan, whilst oppressive in other ways, can empower a woman to access services without the partner preventing her, so clarification of the services she feels are most viable and useful can only make the plan more likely to protect the child/ren.

Usefully, Trevithick (2012) reminds us that to engage a service user we must be mindful not to make questions too complex or irrelevant, and that the timing of the question is important. As discussed in earlier chapters, the use of the ping-pong conversation style is important: forms of clarifying questions are used to keep the conversation going and prompt the service user to share further information. But remember, where a personal conversation will be made up of roughly equal parts of asking and answering questions, within a professional intervention you will be undertaking the role of asking questions if you are information gathering, or providing answers if you are disseminating information. Your professional role will define your communication role.

Interestingly, Trevithick (2012) and Koprowska (2014) have different recommendations about the use of open and closed questions: Trevithick (2012) argues in favour of varying between them, whilst Koprowska (2014) just starts with closed questions. Both are right. The reality of good social work communication is that you need to develop the ability to interpret the individual situation and respond appropriately to best meet the service user's needs. It is also, as is the whole philosophy of this book, about reflecting on your own optimum way of intervening, and working in a way that suits your individual social work style.

Rogers et al. (2016) remind us that *hypothetical* questions are also a good way to clarify wishes and feelings. Utilising the philosophy of solution-focused interventions (De Shazer, 1984), asking the service user the *miracle question* is a good way to gain a clearer understanding of what they want, when perhaps even they do not clearly understand their wishes and feelings.

ACTIVITY 4.3

When you go to sleep tonight, a miracle occurs. When you wake up tomorrow morning, how can you tell that the miracle has happened? How can those close to you tell?

It is likely that your responses will include that you have completed your course and are now a qualified social worker, but may also include a response such as that your children or friends are delighted as they see you more, or a personal response such as that your relationship with a loved one has improved. Remember that as a student social worker undertaking the miracle question with a service user, it is a tool to gather clear information, it is not up to you to judge if this is realistic or achievable: you are still in the information gathering stage. Ask open questions to keep the discussion positive (what they will see as a result of the miracle, as opposed to what is missing) and to clarify details. By looking at the miracle morning from a positive, or strengths-based perspective, you will support the service user to see for themselves what they want and how life could look if they engaged with the intervention: clarifying their wishes and feelings for them too.

Mirroring and paraphrasing

Mirroring is the isolation of a word or phrase that you do not understand and which requires further definition by repeating and accenting, and using it in your question. For example, Clara states that her partner blames her for the domestic abuse, so the student social worker may ask, 'Blames you? In what sort of ways?' Mirroring is a useful technique to further a discussion and gain clarification of detail and understanding. Mirroring can also be helpful to explore the choice of word or phrase, for example why did Clara choose to use the term 'partner' when she states that she is separated from him? Mirroring enables you to clarify the situation.

By contrast, paraphrasing is repeating back the essence of what a person has said in your own words, which helps ensure that you have understood correctly. Paraphrasing can often be used after a period of information sharing by a service user. O'Brien (2016) discusses the Rogerian techniques of *reflecting feeling*, which enables the student social worker to explore further the emotions raised within the discussion by the service user; and *paraphrasing content*, which enables the student social worker to summarise and repeat the details of the discussion, to demonstrate that they had heard and understood what the service user has said.

Paraphrasing also helps the service user hear what they have said, giving them an opportunity to reflect on it. For example, the student social worker may paraphrase a discussion with Clara on the impact of domestic abuse on the children, such as:

'You feel that Matthew's reluctance today to go to school may be linked to your argument last night.' It can also be used to move the discussion on, for example adding an open question, 'Why do you think that might be?'

ACTIVITY 4.4

Ask a peer to talk to you about their weekend. Utilise mirroring questions and then paraphrase the discussion at points.

- How does this feel?
- Is it a natural way to hold a conversation?
- Do you find one easier than another?

Summarising

Summarising can be used at the start of a session to recap a previous discussion or intervention, and during and at the end of an appointment to recap current discussion and development, by outlining the themes discussed, agreed goals and future meetings. This enables you to clarify your perception of the agreed outcome and allows the service user to hear it. This, along with affording the service user a safe opportunity to agree or challenge your perspective, is important in working in a person-centred manner. Egan (2014: 117) suggests that summarising helps the service user see the 'bigger picture'. However, he reminds us to ensure that we summarise the service user's strengths as well as areas for development.

Furthermore, Egan (2014: 117) argues that summarising can also be helpful when a discussion reaches a standstill and needs moving forward, by summarising and asking the service user where they would like to progress from here. And finally, Koprowska (2014) argues that by summarising at the end of a session your case notes will be more concise and easier to write because you have drawn your thoughts together.

ACTIVITY 4.5

Ask a colleague to tell you about their best friend. Let them talk for five minutes, then ask them open and closed questions to develop the conversation. When they finish, summarise what they have said in 30 seconds. Can you identify the key issues?

Clarification shows respect for the service user: you are interested in them, demonstrating active listening, and value them enough to ensure that you have their perspective.

CONGRUENCE

As discussed in Chapter Three on listening, you need to observe and hear both verbal and non-verbal communication. Sometimes there is a congruence between the two, which will indicate that the person's verbal communication is supported by their non-verbal communication, therefore implying that they are being open and honest with themselves and/or you. Drawing attention to a lack of congruence between verbal and non-verbal communication needs to be done without making the person self-conscious, but a gentle clarification of perspective is appropriate. You might ask Clara: 'You smiled when you talked about Jack's difficult behaviour in a morning. How do you feel about him?'

REFLECTIVE TASK 4.2

Start to think about how you feel about using these clarification techniques.

- Which ones are you comfortable with?
- Is there one that you can see you need to develop a little further?

As you move to the communication skills audit at the end of the chapter, this exercise will enable you to develop your action plan for clarification.

CLARIFICATION FOR THE SERVICE USER

Thus far, we have focused on clarification to aid informed decision making. However, we must also consider ensuring that the service user understands what we have said. As a student social worker you have to impart a significant amount of information about choices, services, expectations, entitlements, concerns, rights, legislation, etc., which can be overwhelming for a service user who is feeling scared, threatened or confused. Linking back to our discussion in Chapter Two, people's recent and historical experiences will impact not only on their presentation but also on their ability to hear and to process information. Different people process information differently, with different values, perspectives and understandings. As the social worker, you will have to take account of this and adjust your communication accordingly.

Woodcock Ross (2016) reminds us that being clear in our purpose to the service user is essential in engaging them. As a student social worker, always ensure that your information is correct, clearly presented, and written material is provided where appropriate. You may need to repeat information on consecutive visits and revisit information as your work progresses. Think about cognitive ability, stress levels, language ability or physical impairment: all will impact on a service user's ability to hear or understand your discussion.

CASE STUDY 4.1 REVISITED

Thinking back to Clara, in order to support her to make an informed decision about safeguarding her children, you might tell her that if there are further incidents of domestic abuse, there will be concerns raised at the next child protection conference.

- Do you feel that this is an open and honest discussion or a threatening and intimidating one?
- How do you feel about stating the same to the father/perpetrator?

There is a fine line between giving the service user information to enable them to make an informed choice and a veiled threat. In part, it will depend on where this falls in your intervention. If it is the tenth time that you have raised concerns, and have done so tactfully as you do not wish to further oppress the mother, perhaps a more assertive manner is called for. You will be required to assess the individual situation and communicate accordingly. However, remember: it is your duty to be clear, you will fail the parents if you do not support them to recognise the need for change. Restorative practice (Wachtel, 2005) reflects the philosophy of *high challenge, high support* in the social discipline window (which Chapter Six explains further). It would advocate a clear statement about concerns to all involved to ensure that the service user knows and understands the need for change and consequences of not engaging, and ensure the intervention was coupled with a high level of support to engage the service user in the intervention. Pennell and Koss (2011) argue that engaging the perpetrator is not against a feminist perspective, but instead enhances the likelihood of change within the family. Also, the woman is empowered by understanding the consequences of her choices.

As your appointment progresses, and at the end of a meeting, check with the service user that they have understood the content. A simple 'Have you understood?' may be sufficient, but in many cases if the service user is feeling insecure they may agree to this closed question rather than risk looking inadequate by expressing a lack of comprehension. You will need to balance that against a derogatory or examination style question that demands a repetition of the facts and agreed plan. An open question that asks them their perspective of the discussion will elicit both clarification and show the service user you value them by listening to them.

Also, remember to finish by offering the service user the opportunity to ask questions. 'Is there anything you wanted to check out with me? I know we've talked about a lot of things today.' This will in turn enable the service user to clarify their understanding with you. Always feel confident to say you will check something out, but ensure that you do provide the promised information. This helps you to look human, rather than all-knowing, and trustworthy when you provide the information.

 COMMUNICATION SKILLS AUDIT: CLARIFICATION SKILLS

Finally, reflect on your strengths and areas for development in relation to your clarification skills and identify two or three action points for you to develop (Table 4.1).

Table 4.1   Communication skills audit: clarification skills

	Strengths in clarification	Areas for development	Action points to improve clarification skills
Domain 1 Professionalism			
Domain 2 Values and ethics			
Domain 6 Critical reflection and analysis			
Domain 7 Intervention and skills			

CONCLUSION

Clarification is important because you do not want to misunderstand the service user, or that they misunderstand you. By clarifying, or checking, that your perception of the conversation or agreements made is the same as the service user's, you will prevent future disengagement or confusion and therefore time wastage. Utilise techniques such as mirroring, summarising and open questions to ensure that you empower the service user by hearing and understanding their perspective.

FURTHER READING

Beck, E., Kropf, N. and Blume L.P. (2010) *Social Work and Restorative Justice: Skills for Dialogue, Peace-making and Resolution.* Milton Keynes: Open University Press. Chapter Nine, 'Feminist perspectives on family rights: social work and restorative practices for stopping abuse of women', offers constructive discussion on using restorative practice intervention skills with women who suffer domestic abuse

Llewellyn, A., Agu, L. and Mercer, D. (2015) *Sociology for Social Workers.* Cambridge: Polity Press. Provides excellent insight into the construction of a multitude of presenting issues, so that thought can be given to clarifying why a service user finds themselves in need of intervention.

Woodcock Ross J. (2016) *Specialist Communication for Social Workers.* London: Palgrave Macmillan. Chapter Four deals with clarification skills, but the later chapters provide stimulating discussion for when working with different service user groups.

CHAPTER FIVE

EMPATHY

Links to Knowledge and Skills Statements

Adults: role of social workers working with adults; person-centred practice; direct work with individuals and families; supervision, critical reflection and analysis; professional ethics and leadership

Children's: relationships and effective direct work; communication; role of supervision

INTRODUCTION

This chapter aims to ensure that the reader understands the difference between empathy and sympathy, and the important role that empathy plays in engaging service users, which is critical as a preventative tool to avert further escalation of social work service provision. It will reflect on how you, the student social worker, can ensure that your intervention values and validates the service user. The chapter will conclude with a reflection on the impact of being empathic and emotionally intelligent, and the need for the reader to ensure that they are proactive in remaining emotionally well.

EMPATHY OR SYMPATHY?

> Sympathy is me orientated, empathy is you orientated. (Howe, 2013: 12)

As a student social worker you will talk to people who are experiencing difficult situations, and you will need to respond in a way that shows the service user that you care whilst taking care that the social worker does not become entrenched in the problem with them. Sympathy is when you respond with an emotional response to the service user's emotional distress.

REFLECTIVE TASK 5.1

You are out for lunch with a close friend when she tells you that she has lost her cat, and is feeling bereft as it was her world and her confidante.
How do you react?

It is likely that you will respond with compassion: this is your friend, you probably knew and had feelings for the cat yourself, and may have an emotional response too. At the very least you can see the pain that someone you care for is feeling. It may also stir old personal memories: a family bereavement, a lost pet or a relationship breakdown. You will talk together about the cat, and you will listen to your friend's feelings, offering kind words of sympathy to her to make her feel better, and you will *feel* emotion. This is a good social response to a friend's grief. By expressing your own emotion within the situation you are expressing sympathy. Sympathy is feeling sorry for your friend's grief, identifying with her grief and feeling it too.

REFLECTIVE TASK 5.2

You undertake a home visit to an older lady, and she tells you that she lost her cat, and is feeling bereft as it was her world and her confidante.
How do you react?

The service user's emotional response is just as valid as your friend's reaction, but you do not have a personal attachment to their situation, and she needs a response that is both detached and caring: empathy. You would still talk to her about the cat, listen to her anecdotes and laugh at the funny scrapes it got into. However, whilst you can see the pain that the service user is feeling, you will not share her feelings, as you had no emotional attachment to the cat. It is important that your response is understanding and kind but does not engage *with* the service user's emotional response.

Even if the discussion triggers memories of your own lost cat, family bereavement or relationship breakdown, an empathic response does not identify them and utilise them in the discussion. This is because if you are listening to your own responses and feelings, then you are not listening to the service user's responses and feelings. You risk projecting your feelings onto the service user, and making assumptions about their wishes, feelings and needs that will ultimately prevent you from being able to engage the service user in the intervention. If the feelings that you have mirror the service user's own feelings, then you may begin to over-identify with the service user, which will make it difficult to be objective.

Thinking about Reflective tasks 5.1 and 5.2, can you identify if you thought sympathetically or empathically (Table 5.1)?

Table 5.1 Examples of sympathetic and empathic responses

Sympathetic responses	Empathic responses
I know how you feel	It is clear that has upset you
That must hurt	You clearly miss her. How did you feel?
I went through the same thing, it was awful	That sounds like it has been a difficult time for you
I am so sorry for you	She sounds like a great companion. What do you miss most about her?

The differences are subtle. Empathy is about reflecting the service user's perspective, rather than your own. The skills that we discussed in Chapters Three and Four on listening and clarification, respectively, will be invaluable to develop your empathy skills. You will need to listen to the service user's feelings, and then clarify them in a way that does not engage your emotional response but acknowledges theirs.

Active listening is wasted without empathic responding. (Egan, 2014: 92)

PERSPECTIVES ON EMPATHY

It is recognised that there is no one definition of empathy. Some authors discuss feeling the service user's pain, others discuss recognising and reflecting it. You will need to determine the level of empathy you will use with your service users. Grant and Kinman (2014) offer a pragmatic perspective that empathy should be a *multi-dimensional* intervention, and utilise Davis' (1983, cited in Grant and Kinman, 2014: 27)) model to recommend that empathy should involve *perspective taking*, listening to and understanding how the service user is feeling, underpinned with a healthy balance of *empathic concern*, which is positive, often motivational, emotional impact of the service user's perspective, and *emotional distress* as feeling a negative emotional impact. Grant and Kinman (2014) reiterate the positive value of use of empathy in terms of understanding and engaging a service user. However, they also warn of the negative value of empathic distress, whereby the social worker understands the service user's responses and feelings so well that they feel them for themselves. They find this stressful and debilitating, which inhibits objective involvement, assessment and intervention.

Whilst there are differing perspectives on how far a social worker should feel the service user's emotions, all are agreed that you should hear and acknowledge them. Egan (2014) represents Clark's (2007) philosophy that there are three types of empathy: subjective, objective and interpersonal. Clark suggests that subjective empathy is an acknowledgement that social workers have history and feelings, and will be influenced by them, but only in terms that will enhance their understanding. He argues that objective empathy does this, but also takes account of the wider issues of theoretical knowledge, and that interpersonal empathy is empathy where the social worker sees the feelings *as if* they were the service user. Howe (2013) approaches it slightly different, and argues that to be an empathic student social worker you will need to combine *cognitive empathy*, where you will reflect on how the service user is feeling by analysing their verbal and non-verbal communication, and *affective empathy*, where you have a sense of (and he argues may feel) your service user's emotional response, which you will be required to *communicate* to the service user.

But more than any perspective, Grant and Kinman (2014) reflect that it is important for a social worker to ensure that they utilise *accurate empathy*. The ability to listen to, understand and reflect back the service user's feelings, so that the service user feels that what they feel has been heard and understood and valued is critical.

REFLECTIVE TASK 5.3

Look back to Chapter One and use Gibbs' reflective cycle to reflect on the loss of the service user's cat.

- What were your reactions? (Evaluation section)
- Were they empathic concerns or empathic distress?
- How do you feel that the service user would have reacted to both of these? (Analysis Section)
- Now, devise an action plan: how would you react to ensure that you displayed accurate empathy?

Developing your empathic skills can be seen to be preventative in nature. If you use empathy, you are more likely to engage the service user. If you engage the service user, you are more likely to be able to support them effectively to address the concerns that you have as a social worker. If you empower the service user to address the concerns, they are less likely to need escalated service provision, so your empathic response has been preventative.

THE SKILLS OF EMPATHY

Ingram (2013) argues that empathy is the foundation of developing a good work-ing relationship with service users. If we reflect back to Hennessey's (2011) discussion on the importance of relationship-based social work in Chapter One, we can see that empathy is an excellent way to develop relationships, by showing that you have heard and understand their perspective. Howe (2013) recognises that as human beings we try to make connections with each other. If a new acquaintance listens to you and asks open questions to further your conversation, you are likely to engage with them more than with an uninterested person. In turn, and returning to the ping-pong conversation analogy in Chapter Three, you will ask questions to engage the service user and the relationship will develop. Howe (2013) believes that human beings instinctively assess each other, analyse this information and respond to them in the optimum way. In social work you will need to harness that instinctive ability and take it a step further. You will be required to demonstrate the interest and assess and analyse the service user's feel-ings, but you will not receive (or be able to respond to) reciprocal advances.

Koprowska (2014) reminds us that empathy is firstly about *recognising* the service user's emotional state. She argues that as a student social worker you need to listen to the service user's words, and also read their non-verbal com-munication, to develop a hypothesis of their emotional response to the event they are describing. Secondly, Egan (2014) argues that the empathic student social worker should then become a *thoughtful processor*. In many ways this is similar to the discussion in Chapter Ten on evidence-based assessments: you should reflect on the service user's wishes and feelings, whilst taking into account any incongruent non-verbal communication that you observe, incorporate your knowledge and understanding of the service user's history, and apply knowledge from your social work experience, theory and research to inform your analysis of the service user's emotional state. The difference, of course, is that with a written assessment the analysis can be written with time to reflect. In a communication situation, this must be done in a spilt second and without losing track of the ongoing discussion! No easy feat.

Having assessed the service user's emotional state, Koprowska (2014) argues that an empathic response should be congruent with the service user's emotional level. This does not mean that if they are angry you should be too, but that if they are very angry you should express recognition of that level of feeling in your empathic mirror response. She argues that a response that minimises the service user's feelings does not acknowledge and value them. Egan (2014) reminds us to ensure that our non-verbal empathic communication mirrors our verbal empathy, as service users will read both elements to validate our sincerity. At this point it is important to remember that empathy can be communicated through a physical touch, such as a hand on a shoulder or forearm, or by a soft glance or eye contact that says: 'I am here with you.' Howe (2013) recognises that a respectful silence also communicates empathy: an understanding that the service user needs a moment to reflect.

ACTIVITY 5.1

In a pair, one person talks about a difficult experience for them. The 'listener' should demonstrate that they are listening empathically through only non-verbal communication: nods, touch and silence.

- Does this feel natural? Of course, in real communication it would supplement verbal communication and not replace it. Try the activity again using both verbal and non-verbal communication.
- How does it feel as the person who is being talked to: did you feel valued?

Shulman (2012) recognises the importance of empathy throughout the working relationship with a service user. In Chapter Two, we discussed *preparatory empathy*, which Shulman (2012) reflects is thinking about how the service user might be feeling in meeting you for the first time. Furthermore, he talks about *tuning in*, as a way of the student social worker identifying the feelings and issues that the service user may have and the impact that they will have on their ability to engage and begin the process. Trevithick (2011) supports this argument when she analyses the impact of a service user's defensive behaviours on their presentation, and the importance of understanding this as a student social worker and utilising creative responses to engage the service user. Shulman (2012) continues that the student social worker must *tune in* to the unspoken agenda of the service user has as assessment and intervention continue, for example identifying patterns of behaviour that indicate an issue, or the service user's unspoken or suppressed feelings.

Shulman (2012) argues that before a student social worker can understand the service user's feelings, they must be aware of, or *tuned into*, their own feelings. Shulman (2012) argues that it is only by demonstrating this understanding to the service user (through emotionally intelligent, empathic verbal and non-verbal support) that they can feel safe to explore their own feelings and the intervention will be successful. It follows, then, that in order to be empathic, you must reflect on your own feelings and experiences to give you emotional intelligence.

CASE STUDY 5.1

Egan (2014) recommends that empathy is enhanced by:

- Giving yourself time to think
- Using short responses
- Reflecting the service user's feelings, but remaining yourself

Go back to the case studies in previous chapters of this book. Imagine that the service user or student is telling you their history. In turn, think of an empathic response to each of them.

- Chapter One: Aisha's home visit that results in her sharing personal details with a service user
- Chapter Two: Mr Olikara tells you his history as an asylum seeker
- Chapter Three: Harriet's experiences of hate crime as a result of her learning difficulty.
- Chapter Three: Mr Cook's anxiety about being discharged from hospital to live at home alone and his desire to be more active.
- Chapter Three: Isabelle's demand to be accommodated by the local authority
- Chapter Four: Clara's recounting the incident of domestic abuse

Do you feel more confident as you develop this skill? Remember: you are looking for a response that represents their perspective on how they may feel (not your own), one that still represents your style of communication but one that reflects a concise summary of their feelings.

Howe (2013) reflects on the ability to develop empathy. He recommends, based on research with medical students, that empathy can be developed by reading case scenarios and reflecting on the patient's perspective. He also reflects that watching videos containing aggression and reflecting on how the victim may feel develops empathy. Similar to this, research by Konrath et al. (2015) suggests that one can develop empathy through reflection on daily text prompts. The key theme seems to be exposure to emotional issues and practising your responses.

ACTIVITY 5.2

Identify a character in a television soap opera such as *Coronation Street*. Imagine that the character is telling you their history. Think of an empathic response in turn to each of their significant story lines.

Grant and Kinman (2014) recommend the use of role play in supervision as preparation for a home visit, meeting or office appointment, to develop a student social worker's empathic responses. Reflecting on the phrase 'practise makes perfect', practising to be empathic does develop your skill and enhance your ability. Van Berkhout and Malouff (2016) analysed empathy training and found that undertaking and reflecting on a combination of experiential role plays, lectures and case studies was the most productive way to enhance empathy in professional education. The moral here is to embrace the varied learning opportunities that you are offered.

THE BENEFITS OF UTILISING EMPATHY

Engaging service users

As social workers, we are often faced with talking to service users who are in difficult situations, often in times of crisis. This may be compounded by the arrival of a social worker: you. Empathy is a non-condescending, non-judgemental way to engage the reluctant-to-engage service user. It does not assume that you know how a service user will feel or react, but that you value their individual feelings and reactions: a very person-centred way to respond to service user's feelings. If you can convey an understanding of their perception of the situation, then the service user will feel more supported and valued, and be more likely to engage with you. Egan (2014) argues that people just want to be understood, and that when this is experienced by a service user, it is a powerful event. The acknowledgement by a professional of their feelings can validate the service user, making them feel valued. Empathy can build a positive foundation from which to build your relationship. This is not to say that one empathic statement will ensure service user engagement, but that it can establish a working relationship to build from with other positive social work practices.

Howe (2013) recognises that by engaging the service user with empathy, they will feel safe and ready to explore their situation. That is, empathy is a step beyond clarification, not just a summary of what has just been said, but also a prompt or stimulation to continue the discussion. As a student social worker you can only benefit from greater understanding of the service user's situation, which may lead to them identifying problems and triggers, and being able to implement changes or coping strategies. You will need to practise empathic communication as a student, but be aware that false empathy or clichés can be counter-productive and alienate the service user further.

Anti-oppressive practice

Like listening, empathy needs to be non-judgemental. You will need to reflect the service user's feelings without prejudice. As with listening, you will be able to reflect on their content after the meeting, and the impact on your decision making, but at the time, you are just a mirror reflecting their feelings.

Howe (2013) recognises that there may be ethno-cultural empathy, that is, one is more likely to be more empathic to a service user of similar ethnic or cultural background. This is supported by further research, including that by Neumann et al. (2013). Nevertheless, Egan (2014) argues that a benefit of empathic communication is that it enables the culturally – or to extend it further age, gender, class, etc. – mismatched social worker and service user to understand each other. If a young male student social worker is able to assess how the older female service user in Reflective Task 5.2 feels and uses empathic responses to demonstrate that he understands her loss, then she is more likely to engage with him. As such, it is critical that we actively listen to the service user to hear their wishes, feelings and needs, to ensure that we can be empathic.

Myers (2008) reflects that it is a difficult task to develop the ability to recognise your emotional reaction to a social work intervention, yet to respond in a non-judgemental way. Revisting the Chapter One discussion on Schön's (1983) reflection in action, practice requires reflection and clear emotional intelligence, and awareness of your feelings and prejudices to be able to communicate effectively, appropriately and empathically.

REFLECTIVE TASK 5.4

Do you need to have been abused to listen to a child who felt they had?

Very few of you will have experienced this level of traumatic childhood. But it is not expected that you should have, as hearing the service user's experience is key to empathy. Nevertheless, children's social workers are often accused of not being able to understand if they do not have children of their own (assumptions can be made about the social worker's personal circumstances). As social workers we do not need to have experienced a service user's difficulty to support them. We need to hear their account of *their* experiences. Empathy enables us to show the service user that we have done so.

Emotional competence

Thinking back to Chapter One, you were asked to reflect on your emotional competence, your ability to reflect and how you would develop your communication skills. Grant and Kinman (2014) recommend empathic reflection in order to achieve accurate empathy. They argue that reflection can support a student social worker to consider their emotional responses to a service user, both the causes and the impact of them, which will enable the student social worker to develop better empathic responses. They also argue that reflection develops the skill of understanding how and why a service user may be feeling and reacting in a certain way, another key skill in both being empathic, and emotionally intelligent. Indeed, they cite Grant's earlier research (2014), which concluded that reflection led to improved empathic communication. Koprowska (2014) reminds us of the positive impact on our emotional wellbeing in empathic interventions. Wagaman et al. (2015) undertook research into the impact of empathic interventions and concluded that social workers who used empathic communication may be less likely to suffer from stress and burnout. Furthermore, they were also more likely to increase their *compassion satisfaction*. The authors argued, drawing on Stamm's (2010, cited in Wagaman et al., 2015: 201) work, that compassion satisfaction is an initial positive belief that the service user can make changes, so the social worker is more likely to come from a strengths-based perspective. The empathic student social worker is more likely to be motivated and committed to a positive outcome for the service user, and will take positive energy from a successful service user outcome: clearly a positive cycle to be in for both student social worker and service user, as well as the employer, as they argued staff retention was also improved.

Nevertheless, Howe (2013) reflected that whilst we can develop empathy skills, it will be difficult to remain empathic at all times. Our mood, workload, personality match or clash, and unconscious biases will impact on our ability to be effectively empathic. He reminds us that we need to be mentally healthy to be empathic, otherwise we can become too self-absorbed and barriers to communication (see Chapter Eight) will prevent us from being empathic. Obviously, the need to be emotionally intelligent becomes apparent at this juncture, as we need to be aware when outside forces are impeding our ability to be successfully empathic.

Grant (2014) reminds us that as empathic social workers we need to be mindful that we do not become overly engaged with our service user's emotional responses. It is therefore important that as a student social worker who practises empathic communication that you are aware of the impact of your personal experiences and do not negate them. Instead, explore them in an emotionally intelligent supervision to support your understanding of them. She suggests that reflective practitioners are more likely to be accurately empathic, with less negative side effects of over-identifying with the service user's emotions and eventually suffering stress and ultimately burnout. So, as you develop as a student and qualified social worker, the key to successful interventions is to be open to discussing the feelings that you encounter to ensure that they do not impact on your communication skills.

Ingram (2013) concurs with Munro's (2011) report, both recommending that social workers need to acknowledge that an emotionally empathic response not only engages the service user in assessment and intervention but also reduces stress and emotional toil for them. You will need to continue to be proactive in developing and maintaining your ability to be empathic as your social work career develops.

COMMUNICATION SKILLS AUDIT: EMPATHY SKILLS

Finally, reflect on your strengths and areas for development in relation to your ability to be empathic and identify two or three action points for you to develop (Table 5.2).

Table 5.2   Communication skills audit: empathy skills

	Strengths in empathy	Areas for development	Action points to improve empathy skills
Domain 2 Values and ethics			
Domain 6 Critical reflection and analysis			
Domain 7 Intervention and skills			

CONCLUSION

In conclusion, the key issue with empathy is not to assume. You need to use your listening skills to hear the service user's perspective and your clarification skills to ensure that you have heard appropriately. Then communicate your understanding through both verbal and non-verbal empathic communication, so that you can support the service user to explore both their feelings and possible outcomes in a person-centred way for optimum engagement.

FURTHER READING

Egan, G. (2014) *The Skilled Helpe: A Client-centred Approach*, 10th edn. Hampshire: Cengage. Chapter Three, 'Empathic presence and responding', provides a therapeutic summary of the importance of utilising empathy, and the skills required to do so.

Howe, D. (2013) *Empathy. What is it and Why it Matters*. Basingstoke, Hampshire: Palgrave Macmillan. This book is a crucial and accessible read to support your understanding of empathy.

CHALLENGING: HOLDING SENSITIVE CONVERSATIONS

Links to Knowledge and Skills Statements

Adults: person-centred practice; safeguarding; effective assessment; direct work with individuals and families; supervision, critical reflection and analysis; professional ethics and leadership

Children's: relationships and effective direct work; communication; adult mental ill health, substance misuse, domestic abuse, physical ill health and disability; child and family assessment; analysis, decision making, planning and review; the role of supervision

INTRODUCTION

This chapter will explore the dynamics of challenging within social work practice encounters and will review the communication skills used to put this into practice. The skill of challenging is a diverse one within the social work profession, as it takes place in many social work contexts, including face to face, direct contacts and during meetings. Indeed the inter-disciplinary nature of the social care profession will require the practitioner to be able to present their point of view and to negotiate plans of care for service users in partnership with many other professionals across the health and social care sector. It is important, then, that the skill of challenging other people's opinions and being able to justify your own judgements is an integral and core part of the role of a social worker (for a fuller discussion of these areas see Chapter Eleven on inter-professional communication).

For the purposes of this discussion, the focus will be on the direct work between the service user and social worker, as it is through these professional conversations that a working alliance takes place through day-to-day contacts. Within social work literature we place these conversations under the generic heading of 'interviewing skills' (Koprowska, 2014). This chapter will outline how to challenge within interviews, what to look for in relation to skills of observation, active listening and interviewing techniques. This will include an exploration of the practitioner's ability to recognise paralanguage, which is the skill of being able to identify the emotions behind language. The discussion will encourage practitioners to consider the issue of timing within social work encounters and when it is appropriate to challenge someone. The discussion will consider the power differentials between worker and service users and some of the consequences and risks that can be a feature of holding sensitive conversations. At times some issues are best approached in a less direct way and drawing on research from counselling disciplines will enable this discussion to give thought to the psychological risks that are present for the service user when in conversation with a social worker. The discussion will conclude with a focus on the importance of critical reflection and ways to work towards avoiding the emotional damage that can occur as part of interviewing. Challenging is part of a repertoire of social work skills and as such it cannot be discussed or applied in isolation, and, as we shall see, in fact it can be dangerous to attempt to do so. Thus as a skill it requires use of all of the tools of communication we have reviewed in this text. Therefore, this chapter should be read in conjunction with the chapters on clarification (Chapter Four), empathy (Chapter Five) and resistance (Chapter Seven) to ensure a holistic perspective is taken.

WHAT HAPPENS WHEN WE CHALLENGE?

Challenging is a form of constructive feedback within a professional helping relationship. It can be utilised as a way to bring to a service user's attention a different perspective on how they are viewing themselves, or a problem they have, or it can illuminate and bring into focus a new external view of these issues with which they may disagree. These different facets which are inherent within challenging demonstrate how powerful a tool it is. It holds the potential for huge personal development through increased insight (which can be a motivator to change). Conversely, if a person is being asked to change it can also present high risks that pose a psychological threat to someone's sense of integrity and personal safety. Being challenged can therefore result in both physical and affective responses, which as practitioners we are able to observe through paying attention to a person's body language. Body language can reveal what a person is thinking about the feedback they have been given; this may have shed new light on the issues faced. It may also have provoked strong emotions including shame, fear and even hostility (Laird, 2014). Laird's research looked at the findings of serious case reviews in child protection cases where a lack of assertive practice (on behalf of social workers) was found, highlighting that social workers did not challenge service users frequently enough and that challenge was often not effective. Challenge was absent even when workers had observed that service users were under stress. This was often because workers felt intimidated or because it was difficult to broach the issues. Within the field of child protection most service users face multiple disadvantages and are parenting in complex circumstances including coping with mental ill health, family violence, and use of alcohol and drugs to levels that present a high risk for children living in homes where these factors are a consistent presence. Forrester and Harwin (2006) found that one-third of child protection cases involved families where parents abused substances. Therefore it is important that social work practitioners are able to recognise the effects of this behaviour within a person's demeanour; alcohol and drugs can lower inhibitions and lead the person to show aggressive behaviour (Laird, 2014). Additionally, service users who have had a history of being maltreated in their own childhood may have a predisposition towards hostility, including showing higher levels of aggression and having lower tolerance levels when attempting to cope with the frustrations of being challenged or receiving feedback about their behaviour or beliefs (Green, 2001, cited in Laird, 2014: 1976).

ACTIVITY 6.1

In a group discussion, irrespective of your perspective, go against the flow of the discussion. Playing 'devil's advocate', challenge the speaker and ask why they feel that way or state an opposite perspective.

- How does that feel?
- How did you phrase your challenge?

Now take a turn at being the one who is challenged in a group discussion.

- How did that feel?
- How did you respond to the challenge?

After completing this exercise you will be able to appreciate that strong emotions can occur when we feel challenged. In real life these challenges are often perceived to be highly stressful conversations. At times this stress can trigger hostile responses, but this remains an under-researched area of social work practice and education. Newhill and Wexler's (1997) research into aggression found that adolescents are more likely to behave in an aggressive and violent way during a challenging conversation: 41% damaging property and 56% participating in psychical attacks. Adult aggressive behaviour was more likely to be shown via the use of threatening behaviour: 29% in the age range 21–29 years and 41% in the 30+ years age group. Newhill and Wexler's findings identified males as more aggressive in their behaviour, in contrast with Littlechild (2003), who found females are more likely to be psychologically aggressive during high-risk child protection interventions. However, Littlechild's research, which was conducted with fieldwork practitioners and managers, acknowledged that this gender bias could be attributed to the predominant focus on mothers in the child protection process rather than on fathers, who were often either hard to engage or absent in the child protection process itself. Therefore, this evidence base from the research literature informs the practitioner of the importance of understanding aspects of a person's identity, personal history (where this is recorded in case records) and the likely effects of hostile responses.

The research indicates the importance of being assertive in such interpersonal encounters and of eliciting the help and support of supervisors to understand and analyse such behaviours in greater detail to be able to plan constructive attempts at holding and sustaining sensitive conversations. It is highly likely that you will need to rehearse and role play interviews to practise broaching difficult topics, that is, to be able to confidently introduce these topics during the interview. Resistance may also be a factor, so several attempts at the conversation may be required to work through such barriers before you are able to hold the service user's attention and hear their views clearly. In such instances it is useful to conduct challenging interviews in conjunction with another colleague who can aid critical reflection in action by acting as an observer and sometimes if appropriate as a facilitator to the discussion.

BALANCING THE AUTHORITY TO CHALLENGE WITHIN A SUPPORTIVE FRAMEWORK

Before we begin to analyse the dynamics of challenging as a form of communication, it is relevant to think about the power differentials that exist between the social work practitioner and service user. Fundamentally the role of the social worker is not a neutral one as it holds within it the values of the profession as well as wider concepts of accountability (Banks, 2009; Dominelli, 2009). Both these espouse principles of respect for difference and autonomy for service users as well as holding more safeguarding functions to keep individuals safe from the harm that they may pose to themselves or to others. Therefore, there is an ethical dimension to the duality of these two positions, which presents moral questions about how to respond to circumstances when things go wrong and require the formal use of these statutory safeguarding and protective functions for adults and children at risk. There are no straightforward ways to respond, indeed Dominelli suggests that these questions 'constantly have to be posed and responded to in specific contexts' (2009: 25). Therefore, inherent within this professional dilemma are intrinsic connections to our ability to draw on our emotional capacity to make sense of and to understand what is happening. We have spent time in this text exploring the use of self-awareness and our emotional intelligence to understand practice encounters because these are required to help us learn from each inter-personal encounter. Indeed within the skill of challenging it could be argued it is fundamentally important to navigate through encounters that require fine tuning and critical reflection in action (Schön, 1983).

The importance of understanding our legal and role and the purpose of the practice encounter is vital towards developing trusting and meaningful working relationships with service users. The many legal powers placed on a statutory social worker require practitioners to challenge, probe and to conduct thorough investigations when an adult or child are thought to be at risk of harm (Brammer, 2014). Members of the public are fully aware of this legal power and most service users fear this when they come into contact with child protection services, thinking this will result in the removal of their child. In Chapter Seven (on resistance) the discussion sets out the similarities between the therapeutic alliance of the counselling relationship and the practice encounters in social work. This literature provides social work education with a respected evidence base, drawing on themes from therapeutic and helping relationships, which inform and can be applied to practice. Other social sciences disciplines, notably the areas of crime, punishment and social justice, offer social work some helpful considerations, especially in relation to how we manage the formal purpose and legal accountabilities of the role. Wachtel and McCold (2001) are critical about the traditional approaches that formal statutory agencies have towards the social control and policing of members of the community who are under surveillance for breaching the moral and social codes of society. They suggest that interventions are punitive and neglecting, and that these approaches usually result in high levels of resistance from service users who disengage from the system. It could be argued that many aspects of social work, where challenging is a key feature, such as when exercising safeguarding functions, often require practitioners to manage ethical tensions of intervention in areas of private life. Indeed the Human Rights Act 1998 recognises this dilemma and provides the framework from which to balance these interventions so that they are proportionate to the concerns expressed (Brammer, 2014). An example of levels of interference into people's personal spaces and privacy is conducting an assessment and asking an older service user about personal care needs and finances in order to establish what the need is and who should pay for it. Additionally, when working with parents where child abuse is suspected, sensitive questions about adult behaviours and attitudes towards the child need to be broached with care and sensitivity. In such practice encounters the social worker will be required to give feedback about the answers given, to probe further and sometimes in the interests of achieving change or securing a safer outcome, they will be required to challenge what is being said.

Wachtel and McCold and (2001) use the principles of restorative practice within everyday practice encounters to achieve change through constructive challenge; this approach reminds the profession of its fundamental values linked to social justice. Wachtel and McCold suggest that practitioners should adopt a four-stage model called the social control window, which offers high challenge from the professional balanced alongside high support plans. In contemporary practice examples, these are typically seen as restorative circles of support around the individual who may be the perpetrator of a crime. Within family support services, these plans are often constructed within the family group conferencing approach, when there are concerns about a child's safety and welfare. Restorative practice recognises the accountability and safety elements of the legal requirements of the role of the social worker. Indeed, these boundaries are made explicit within the working relationship, which begins by making it clear in jargon-free language what the social worker is worried about, why this is a concern and what steps need to be taken to achieve change. Emphasis is placed on seeking to encourage service users to take responsibility for the areas of concern, including increasing their insight into the effects of this on other people. Questioning and challenging is framed in such a way as to elicit in the individual an increased capacity to understand the concerns and to identify what they can do to effect change in their life. This restorative approach is a growing area of practice, providing successful outcomes for service users who are able to be active participants in an intervention that symbolically aims to enable people to achieve change whilst also becoming accountable for their actions towards others. There are six overarching principles to follow when putting this model into practice:

1. *Foster awareness*: Share your own feelings to elicit in the person some insight into how their behaviour/actions make others feel.
2. *Avoid lecturing*: When exposed to other people's feelings, this should promote empathy and renewed insight. Lecturing would likely produce a defensive and blaming response as the person seeks to distance themselves from responsibility.
3. *Involve the person actively*: The person is invited to speak first about their account of events; they are asked to identify solutions, including hearing how other people feel about the events.
4. *Accept ambiguity*: The social worker must recognise that attributing fault is an uncertain process, especially at the start of the work; the emphasis should be on encouraging people to accept as much responsibility as possible.
5. *Separate the deed from the doer*: Value the person overall and only disapprove of the behaviour.
6. *Learn from each conflict*: See mistakes as a valuable tool for personal development.

(Adapted from Wachtel and McCold, 2001: 128)

TECHNIQUES FOR BUILDING CHALLENGING INTO CONVERSATIONS

Restorative approaches to practice are an important framework for the practitioner to adhere too, particularly when facing difficult encounters with service users when challenging is happening. These restorative principles correlate with person-centred practice, which stresses the importance of seeing things from the person's 'own internal frame of reference' (Nelson-Jones, 2016: 49). For example, restating the conversation in terms of how the service user sees things, such as, 'You are feeling annoyed', etc. When attempting to challenge an aspect of someone's behaviour or attitudes, Egan (2014) stresses the importance of inviting the service user to consider discrepancies in their thinking rather than challenging via outright confrontational conversations. He reminds us about the significance of the boundaries of professional relationships: 'shoving the truth down clients' throats usually leads nowhere' (Egan 2014: 150).

Additionally, Nelson-Jones (2016) highlights the importance of getting the timing right in order to be effective in bringing about change when attempting to challenge an issue. He suggests that early on in the relationship, challenges should be delivered in a light way as a more direct approach can result in resistant behaviour. A light way to challenge could be to change the pitch and tone of your voice to show interest or concern in the topic that is being shared. You may also use light humour to query whether if things are really as they appear to be. To help us be prepared for what to expect when challenging, we must accept that, alongside resistance, common reactions to being challenged can include 'discrediting challengers, persuading challengers to change their views, devaluing the issue, seeking support elsewhere … agreeing with the challenge inside helping but then doing nothing about it outside' (Nelson-Jones 2016: 87). These strong affective responses demonstrate the power implicit in being challenged, which can cause a person to feel overwhelmed. Indeed Nelson-Jones cautions professionals against constant challenge, which can 'create an unsafe emotional climate' (Nelson-Jones, 2016: 87). Moreover Egan suggests that a more successful approach is to provide service users with a choice structure, a way of seeing things, from which they are able to challenge their thinking. To put this into practice, Egan gives the example of asking the service user to imagine seeing the problem from another person's perspective such as their partner or child's. This is a useful exercise, in which the service user can be encouraged to identify behaviours and attitudes that are right or need to be reconsidered (Egan 2014). Nelson-Jones (2016) makes a helpful distinction between challenging, which can itself seem to be an aggressive stance and instead favours the use of achieving change through the use of constructive feedback. Feedback maybe used to comment on skills in interactions, behaviours and relationships. The use of 'I' statements are encouraged to show that you as a helper observed this, giving specifics about what you noticed could be changed for the better. When taking this approach towards delivering challenging as a form of constructive feedback, it is helpful to follow the good practice convention of allowing people to self-appraise first. It is always better if someone is able to identify their own issues and to elicit ways this could be changed in future.

CASE STUDY 6.1

Josh, aged 15 years, is looked after in a local authority children's home. He has been living away from his family for two years because of concerns about his mother's parenting and mental ill-health. Josh has begun to stay out late at night and been found drunk by staff on a number of occasions. When challenged about this he is verbally abusive to the staff and has kicked a door, causing damage.

As Josh's social worker you are asked to visit him to talk about these behaviours. Think about how you will approach challenging Josh's attitude towards staff.

Responding sensitively towards adolescent behaviour takes great skill and care, and in real life the benefit of having a relationship with Josh would help you know how to pitch this particular conversation. Imagine two best and worst case scenarios about how Josh might react. If Josh is angry that you have been called in to 'lay down the law' he is likely to be resistant towards attempts to discuss his behaviour. A better approach might be to be more subtle in your challenge by describing the feelings and emotions of concern you and the residential staff felt when Josh was missing. Add in specific detail about concern for him being out in the dark, without money and cold, etc. This will enable you to show an appropriate emotional response that you care about Josh and his wellbeing. You could begin to use 'I' statements to suggest to Josh: 'I wonder what you were thinking at the time you chose not to come home, I imagine that you may have felt angry, sad, annoyed, etc. about …'. This approach might elicit a more open response from which to understand what is happening to Josh, and explore it with him. It is realistic to expect to have to revisit this conversation a number of times before you have been able to explore Josh's safety and the authority's responsibilities towards him.

CASE STUDY 6.2

Carmen and Mick are parents to Ella, 18 months old, and Craig, four years old. The children are subjects of a Children Act 1989 Section 17 children in need plan (sometimes referred to as a common assessment framework (CAF) or by another name locally) because professionals are concerned about neglectful home conditions and a lack of child-centred routines. The parents have found it hard to engage with professionals, and Mick in particular is resistant, often losing his temper when concerns are shared.

Imagine you are at a review meeting when the health visitor challenges the parents because they have not brought the children to a number of important health appointments. Mick explodes at this claiming he is being criticised and storms out of the room. As the lead professional you have to attempt to talk with Mick and ask him to return to the meeting to discuss the concerns.

- Write a few short sentences about what you could say to challenge this behaviour.
- How well do you rate the way the challenge was posed? List what you think was good about this and then explore how you would change this.
- Review your answers using the six points from McCold and Wachtel (2001) as previously discussed.

We have begun to identify the skills the practitioner is applying whilst in the process of creating a safe climate within the conversation from which to incrementally begin to challenge areas that need to be addressed or changed. We have identified that alongside the practitioner's attitudinal position of both the restorative and person-centred approaches, a number of core communication skills begin to interplay to inform and create the space for challenging to occur. For example, observation skills are crucial in order to assist the practitioner to appraise whether the timing is correct and how the person is feeling about what is being said. Through active listening skills as practitioners we use our knowledge of paralanguage to assess the emotional messages the service user is implying during a conversation. Nelson-Jones (2016) calls this the interpretation of inconsistencies, where during the interaction we reflect on the verbal, vocal and body language to read the messages the person is sending. The important interplay of skills here allows the practitioner to hypothesise what the service users really feels about the problem they are facing. This enables the practitioner to establish if this emotion is congruent with what is being said. For example: 'You're telling me you feel sad about it, yet you are smiling' (Nelson-Jones, 2016: 86). Looking for and acting on inconsistencies is recognising the difference between words and actions. It also enables the social worker to challenge the service user's belief in what they value and their underlying commitment to change, through the demonstration of concrete actions. For example, the social worker will make space during the interview to review how the service user has put change into action since the last meeting. Think of a service user who has a dependency on alcohol and who has committed not to drink whilst caring for their child. We would have to challenge the evidence that this promise has been broken, which might include sharing feedback from other people who reported seeing the person under the influence of alcohol, or the child may have talked to you about this, or there may also be evidence of drinking in the home, including running out of finances. In thinking about how to phrase a challenge, Nelson-Jones suggests that verbal messages can start with 'on the one hand … on the other … but …' or 'I'm getting mixed messages' (2016: 86). In addition, Shulman (2016) highlights the importance of being able to identify when people cannot stay on focus and are resisting addressing a difficult issue. He says that people fill the space by either talking a lot around the issues of concern or use silence to avoid talking about the problem. Silence if left unchallenged can become a fixed state (see Chapter Seven for further discussion). It is up to the worker to address this through a subtle challenge that brings the issue out into the open. One example could be: 'You seem to be saying a lot about how you feel about your work, when it is really your relationship with your son that is worrying you. You seem to be avoiding this – is it because you feel it is too painful to talk about?'

CASE STUDY 6.3

Dionne misuses drugs and, as a result of the impact of this on her parenting, her children are being looked after by the local authority. She informs you that she has reduced her drug use and would like the children to be returned to her care, but a drug test contradicts this assertion, and the current plan is for longer period of assessment whilst the children remain in a foster placement.

- How will you raise the difference between Dionne's verbal report and drug test result with her?
- How will you discuss the local authority's perspective that the children should remain looked after?
- Practise holding this conversation with a peer/colleague to establish what you will say.
- How well do you rate the way the challenge was posed?
- List what you think was good about this and then explore how you would change this.

As social workers we often have to talk to people about sensitive subjects or taboo issues, such as sexual behaviour, personal care needs, death, dying and loss. Shulman (2016) highlights that, when doing so, it is important for the service user to feel safe and therefore they need verbal encouragement and reassurance from the practitioner about how difficult it is to share such issues. In such instances the practitioner must take the lead and acknowledge this, for example, there may be an aspect of your identity such as gender, age or cultural differences that adds to the person's feelings of embarrassment. It is important that you address this early on so that it is not a barrier to engagement: just acknowledging how difficult it is to share sensitive information is an important starting position.

Suoninen and Jokinen (2005: 417) discuss the use of 'persuasive questions' as a more indirect way to provide constructive feedback to service users and suggest that, in contemporary social work practice, goal-orientated approaches are 'embedded' within interviewing techniques. We can see an example of this within motivational interviewing, which is a popular goal-directed way of problem solving to achieve behaviour change. Motivational interviewing is based on the premise that the service user has the innate ability to bring about change through facilitative questions directed by the helper, who searches for optimistic ways to encourage the person to think about how they can achieve their goals (Healy, 2014). Suoninen and Jokinen (2005) identify four themes within social work interviewing techniques. Firstly, persuasive questioning, which is a question from the practitioner phrased in a way that hints at and provides suggestions over the best course of action the service user should take to address their problem. Secondly, within this approach is a strong suggestion the practitioner can give in directing the service user towards the right answer, through giving persuasive responses to the information that is given. The service user may choose not to pick up on these suggestions or may take cues from the worker on how responsive they are to the answers they provide. Thirdly, the practitioner can also ask probing questions using clarification techniques. Fourthly, encouraging questions can be used, which can subtly persuade the service user to reconsider their position. Suoninen and Jokinen (2005: 483) comment that the interplay of these themes will be present within all interviews in diverse and unpredictable ways. Because of this they stress the importance of questioning styles being used in fluid and responsive ways that reflect the service user's reactions and own inner account of their difficulties. Being conscious of and alert to these changes within the interview is essential as this will steer the practitioner on how to phrase the next question, including making a judgement over how directive, i.e. challenging or subtle, this should be. However, while concurring with the themes outlined above, Hall and Slembrouck sound a note of caution, as they view advice giving as a form of social control and favour instead a shared approach to build on incremental steps towards 'constructed agreements' (2013: 106) within interviews rather than seeing service users as passive recipients of professional advice. Thompson (2015a) also makes the distinction between seeking to persuade others and manipulation, which clearly runs contrary to the emancipatory values of the social work profession (Banks, 2009). For Thompson, persuasion as a form of influence should result in both sides coming away from an encounter in a winning/positive position. This is best achieved by giving clear constructive feedback including being clear about what your concerns are, and using listening skills and empathic attunement towards the service user's concerns.

REFLECTIVE TASK 6.1

Think of a practice encounter you have had where you have sought to persuade and influence the other person. If you are yet to go into practice, think of an occasion when you have had to challenge a friend or relative about their attitude or behaviour which you found offensive. How did you feel about taking this approach?

Ask a colleague or supervisor to observe your skills in challenging, focusing on the statements you used to share the inconsistencies in the service user's behaviour, language and narrative.

COMMUNICATION SKILLS AUDIT: CHALLENGING

Finally, reflect on your strengths and areas for development in relation to challenging and identify two or three action points for you to develop (Table 6.1).

Table 6.1   Communication skills audit: challenging

	Strengths at challenging	Areas for development	Action points to improve your ability to challenge
Domain 1 Professionalism			
Domain 3 Diversity			
Domain 5 Knowledge			

	Strengths at challenging	Areas for development	Action points to improve your ability to challenge
Domain 6 Critical reflection and analysis			
Domain 7 Intervention and skills			

CONCLUSION

In this chapter, we have considered some of the aspects of social work interviews where challenging is necessary. We have reviewed the principles of restorative practice that offer the ability to create a safer working alliance between the practitioner and service user. These principles show that high challenge must sit alongside high support plans, which together can offer creative practice and a more realistic attempt towards promoting personal development for individuals and family groups. We have thought about inequalities and disadvantages such as adverse life experiences that service users may have had in early life, which could predispose them towards showing high sensitivity in responses when challenged. Additionally, we recognised the significance of being alert to and informed about the effects of alcohol and drugs on a person's behaviour, in order to approach challenging in a safe and planned way. We have explored the timing of challenging and how to find the right space in the conversation to build in indirect and subtle challenges. As the evidence suggests, this is most likely to be more effective because it elicits personal disclosure from the person about their motivation to change. We have been able to make links between challenging and resistance that co-exist within encounters where sensitive conversations are happening. We have recognised that the social worker needs to be assertive, to share their concerns clearly and simply, including the purpose and power of the social work role. We have reviewed statements and questions, to show how to frame language in a way that is constructive towards tapping into service users' true emotions about their concerns and to elicit from them their beliefs about the issues of concern. Finally, we have highlighted the responsive and dynamic nature of challenging, which is reflexive to the live scene, the here and now context in which the encounter takes place. To fully understand and to learn from such encounters takes courage, openness and a willingness to learn using critical reflection and support from colleagues and also through evaluating feedback from service users and carers.

FURTHER READING

Mantell, A. (2013) *Skills for Social Work Practice*. London: Sage. Chapter Ten, 'Negotiation skills', considers the important skill of challenging assertively and sensitively.

Mumby, J. (2016) In the Matter of D (A Child) (no. 3). Available at: www.judiciary.gov.uk/wp-content/uploads/2016/01/re-d-a-child-3.pdf (accessed 15 March 2017). For an excellent account of social work practice that uses 'I' statements to express concerns, read the letter written to parents as part of the care proceedings that express concerns for the child.

WORKING WITH RESISTANCE

Links to Knowledge and Skills Statements

Adults: person-centred practice, safeguarding, effective assessment, direct work with individuals and families, supervision, critical reflection and analysis, professional ethics and leadership

Children's: relationships and effective direct work; communication; adult mental ill health, substance misuse, domestic abuse, physical ill health and disability; child and family assessment; analysis, decision making, planning and review; role of supervision

INTRODUCTION

In this chapter we will focus on exploring the dynamics of resistance in working relationships. This is a way of describing what happens between a practitioner and service user when the service user is reluctant to work with the social worker on the areas of their life that people have concerns about. Resistance can be present when despite best efforts to hold engaging conversations, they are thwarted in some way and agreeing a way forward can be very difficult. Another way to think about resistant behaviours is to recognise this as a position a person assumes when they are unwilling or are psychologically unable to be open to the dialogue that is being presented to them. In relation to social work contacts this can happen during any stage of an interaction with a service user. It can be encountered at the beginning of the relationship, or later it can present in more established relationships, where the resistance can be more subtle and covert, revealing more entrenched and unhelpful patterns of behaviour. When the latter occurs, this can result in the practitioner and the service user repeating unproductive conversations, which can lead to both parties feeling confused about why things are not improving. In order to explore what could be taking place in such encounters, we will begin by identifying some of the facets of resistant behaviour to enable you to relate this to your own practice experiences. An analysis of some of the frameworks as to why resistant behaviour occurs will be discussed, so that we can consider measures for more assertive and directive responses from the practitioner to manage this difficult area of social work practice.

Resistance can be both an attitudinal and a behavioural response. It is a way of expressing strong emotions that are often exhibited at times of high stress when people feel under threat. This could be as a result of their personal autonomy, or someone they love and care for, being compromised or coerced in some way. Resistant behaviour is commonly experienced when an outside agency, such as a social worker or another authority figure, expresses concern for a person's behaviour, either towards themselves or others, and they find it difficult to take responsibility for it. In social work this will often mean we have to ask personal information about people's use of alcohol or drugs, their parenting skills or how they manage arguments in their personal relationships. Usually we ask these questions because there has been some information that suggests there is a risk to the person's own wellbeing or that they are a risk towards someone else. A common response to such encounters is to resist discussing these private matters and a feeling of shock or loss of control that aspects of your private life are being questioned. Taylor (2011) and Ekman (2004) offer a helpful position from which to explore 'what' happens when people show resistance as well as going on to consider 'why' people react in this way. They suggest that resistant behaviours are part of our unconscious biological conditioning called the 'fight or flight response', which acts innately as an autoappraiser. This is the automatic unconscious mechanism we use to make sense of what we see and feel when under stress that triggers an emotional response. This fight or flight mechanism automatically takes over our physical self and influences our behaviour when we experience feelings of fear, loss of control and personal crises.

ACTIVITY 7.1

Take a moment to pause here and consider a time when you have felt the power of the 'fight or flight response' in your own life. Think about the context of what was happening for you and the people around you.

(Continued)

(Continued)

- How did you behave when you felt cornered into something or coerced?
- How do you feel you dealt with this situation?
- Do you prefer fight, flight or resolution?

This can be a difficult reflective task to complete; however, its purpose here is to enable you to access authentic emotions, which then will allow you to think empathetically towards a person who is experiencing the fight or flight response.

For many of us, the attitudinal feelings will be easy to tap into and to recall – the scene may be a powerful memory of times in life when we have felt compromised, shamed and fearful. With some distance from the event, we no doubt move towards a more conscious critical understanding of our own as well as other people's behaviour to be able to articulate why this happened. This sense of distance encourages us to reflect on our actions (Schön, 1983). Therefore, when you are encountering resistance it is essential to seek agency support through a supervisory relationship. Within this space you will be able to explore and analyse what is happening to better understand the message the service user is sending through their behaviour.

ACTIVITY 7.2

Think of an encounter you have had with a friend or colleague when they have spoken disrespectfully to you.

- How did you react to this?
- What is your natural disposition towards conflict?
- Do you appease, resolve or challenge?

Egan referred to resistance as the shadow side of helping: 'because clients don't talk about these feelings, and they are only apparent by analysing a client's behaviour and communication (or lack thereof)' (2002: 171).

Egan (2002) and Shulman (2016) identify several behaviours that may be recognisable to practitioners to help identify resistance that can manifest as belligerence, dismissiveness or coning. These behaviours may be a signal of feeling out of control or of being coerced, and sometimes these unconscious, strong emotions can show themselves as aggression. In contemporary times the language used to talk about service users at the political and social level is full of negative connotations, for example families are called 'troubled', young people are seen as 'out of control', the unemployed as 'lazy scroungers' and people with substance misuse are labelled as 'druggies'. These can be a powerful contribution towards a service user's fear of working with you. Therefore, within your role as a social worker, it is important to build authentic rapport quickly with the person you are trying to support. The best way to achieve this is to have a clear sense of purpose about your role and to explain your concerns clearly at the beginning of the encounter. Trotter terms this purpose setting as the duality between the roles of authority and helper, and suggests a way to clarify your role is to say 'what are we here for?' (2006: 21). The social worker must be able to express their concerns by succinctly and clearly saying 'I am worried about this because …'.

REFLECTIVE TASK 7.1

Think of a time when you have been challenged or belittled by a person in authority (this could be anyone who has had an important role in your life, such as a teacher, tutor or doctor). Also think about a time when you have been supported by a person in power.

- Which of these two memories were more positive for you?
- Reflect on the skills that the supportive person utilised. What can you adopt from them and their approach to help you engage and support service users?

REFLECTIVE TASK 7.2

Imagine that a social worker rings you and asks to visit immediately. They arrive at your house and start asking you questions and criticising your parenting. They state that your child's school has raised concerns, but the school has not raised this with you.

- How do you feel? Angry, shocked, numb, incandescent with rage?
- How would you express those feelings?
- Would you feel able to answer the questions that the social worker was asking?

Next imagine you are the social worker knocking on the door. How are you going to cope with the service user's feelings of anger, rage, shock and surprise? What strategies can you think of that might help during this encounter?

The challenge for you as a worker when facing resistance is to try to maintain rapport and to turn the conversation back onto a reciprocal basis. There are two main ways that resistance and conflict are shown. Firstly, the person can show overt resistance, which can include behaviours such as shouting, violence, denying the concerns and walking away. One way to approach this within the conversation might be to initially allow some time to see if these behaviours settle, effectively giving the person an opportunity to vent their anger, to get their point across and to feel heard. However, if this persists unnecessarily or is repetitive, you might try saying, 'We are here to talk about X. While you are shouting we can't do that. I know that talking about X is important to you, so let's do that now' or 'I can't talk about X while you are shouting. When you are ready we can begin to do this together.' Secondly, passive resistance may present as giving minimal responses such as 'Hmm' and 'Yes' with no genuine commitment being given to the work required to achieve change. It is important to verbalise how you feel about this level of commitment, attempting to look for aspects of the behaviour or the problem that the person is willing to talk more openly about.

CASE STUDY 7.1

Maria Cain (33) is a single carer to her three children, Mark (14), David (11) and Megan (8). The children's father, Michael, left the family home three years ago due to concerns about domestic abuse. He has intermittent contact with the children and often promises to spend time with them but fails to show up for family visits. This is the source of family conflict between the children and their mother, as Maria often criticises Michael to the boys, which leads to significant arguments between Maria and Mark, as he idolises his absent father. Mark displays angry and aggressive behaviour, shouts at Maria and has physically pushed her during these disputes. On one occasion, the neighbours called the police and this resulted in the family being referred to social care for family support. During the early sessions of this work, Maria is very vocal about Mark's attitude and clearly blames him for the arguments. She reports that Mark is out of control, that she can no longer get him up for school as he refuses to go, and she believes it would be better if he lived with his Dad. Mark attends the session, but sits in silence, refusing to talk about how he feels about his relationships. He leaves abruptly when his mother begins to share her feelings.

- Thinking about the dynamics of this family, what signs of resistant behaviour can you identify for Maria and Mark?
- How might you approach working with this family?
- What can you suggest to attempt to alleviate this level of conflict?

You may identify that Maria is angry at the loss of or abandonment by her partner, and that she sees similarities between Michael and Mark, and so transfers her feelings on to him. You may identify that Mark is missing his Dad and feels angry when his Mum criticises him. This links back to your reflections on preparatory empathy in Chapter Two, understanding how the service user might be feeling, so that you can plan the most appropriate intervention.

As part of your journey towards training to be a social worker and during your career you will encounter some of the behaviours we have described so far. Indeed, you may accept that they are reactions to be expected when statutory powers are being used in someone's life. Sometimes this distress or unhappiness is shown as silence, which can act as an expression of non-engagement that can be difficult to work through. Raitakari refers to the use of total silence (Raitakari, 2006, cited in Juhila, 2013: 121), which at times can be a powerful passive act that sends out a 'loud' message to the worker. In such instances, it can be a way a person attempts to keep in control, to dominate the interaction by ignoring all attempts the worker makes to get them to speak. Trevithick (2006) comments that it is important to acknowledge the two-sided nature of silence in which both parties, worker and service user, play an active role. Our ability to tolerate or to react to silence will reveal our own levels of comfort as well as aspects of our identity. For example, in British culture the use of silence could commonly be interpreted as impolite and disrespectful. Trevithick cautions practitioners to monitor their tolerance levels towards silence, as well as their ability to understand whether the silence is being used as a genuine place to gather thoughts or conversely as 'troubled silence' (2006: 176), which may reveal feelings of defensiveness and self-protection. The service user might resist the plans the professional wishes to make, indeed the service user may resist the notion of themselves as needing help and question the methods of intervention in an effort to sabotage the interaction. Nelson-Jones (2016) stresses the importance of the practitioner being transparent about such reluctance to engage. He suggest that the practitioner should confidently reflect back the feelings and the emotions the service users is sending out because 'showing helpees that you understand their internal frame of reference, especially if done consistently, can diminish resistances' (Nelson-Jones, 2016: 97). You might say, 'I am wondering what you are thinking about? Is it because this is frightening? I am thinking possibly that you may feel unhappy about this or with me for asking about this today.'

CASE STUDY 7.1 CONTINUED

In this scenario we have two different expressions of resistant behaviour. In Maria, the mother, we can see shouting and blaming others as a way of resisting addressing feelings of loss of control and fear. In Mark, the son, we can see silence leading to explosive moments of loss of temper and anger at feelings of loss, lack of self-worth and separation from his father.

How might we attempt to engage each person in conversations to begin working through their relationship?

There are no right or wrong answers to this scenario, in real life you will have the benefit of using all of your interpersonal skills to work through such encounters. Sometimes your attempts will be successful and people will open up and share their emotions with you. On other occasions, you will need to be persistent, showing you care enough about the problem to stay with the conversation to try to reach a shared understanding of what is happening. Below, we offer some suggestions of how to work through resistance using the frameworks we have discussed so far.

Maria: The mother is resistant to seeing other people's point of view. You might explain to Maria it is not helpful to blame Mark and to be so vocal in front of him, asking her to think about how this may make him feel. You could separate mother and son and explore feelings, suggesting to Maria that she feels frightened and out of control, and afraid that Mark is following his father. You could work on boundaries with Maria, asking her to agree not to call Dad names in front of the children, explaining that this may make them feel bad about themselves. You could ask Maria not to draw Mark into a conflict by shouting at him when things go wrong. You could begin to work on strategies whereby Maria rehearses more assertive and positive statements to ask Mark to co-operate with family rules and to treat everyone with respect.

Mark: To engage this young person, you could begin by acknowledging that he and his family have been through difficult times and that he must miss his father. You could suggest that this silence is his way of saying 'I am angry and sad about all of this'. You could use 'I' statements to offer suggestions reframing how he might be feeling, such as, 'I am unhappy and it's unfair that I get the blame when it's not my fault.' You could ask him about the ways he has tried to tell his parents about his feelings, asking if that was working for him? You could suggest trying another way. You could tell Mark that workers are supporting them as a family and have asked Maria to be more respectful of Mark's feelings. You could work with Mark on recognising and controlling his anger. You could ask him to take responsibility of getting up for school by tapping into his future goals and aspirations (for example, Mark is a good footballer but lost his place in the school team due to lack of attendance; the teacher is prepared to let him try out for the team again if his attendance improves). You could begin to work on helping Mark to share his feelings and giving him de-escalation techniques to help control his anger. You could attempt to work with Michael, the father, to establish contact and explore his commitment to his relationship with the children.

The strategies we have outlined above for the Cain family are illustrative of Nelson-Jones' (2016) approach towards engaging people at times of distress and working through resistance. He advocates the following: *join with the client*, identify with their concerns to sustain the relationship and extend the conversation hopefully to move this on. Through the positive use of active listening *give permission to discuss reluctance and fears*. *Invite co-operation*, aiming to create an equal partnership. This is an important part of the interaction as it sends a powerful message that the practitioner values the service user's emotions and their point of view. Having addressed this, the practitioner can move on to *enlist self-interest* – this is seeking to encourage the service user to think about what they can gain from attempting to make changes in their life. This latter stage encourages thinking about future possibilities, which could feature positive changes, and can reveal the first insights into the service user's goals and desires (Nelson-Jones 2016). It is important to aim to be an assertive and authoritative practitioner, and Ferguson (2011) terms engaging in this way as using 'good authority' in practice situations. This requires practitioners to critically reflect on their practice to ensure they are achieving a good balance between holding empathic emotional responses with service users whilst also having meaningful and purposeful interactions that seek to improve the circumstances of the service user's life in useful and safe ways. Being assertive in our role is significant and it helps us avoid becoming stuck in repeated patterns of unhelpful attempts to engage service users. It is a skill that we can learn and foster through practice. It is important to be clear about our purpose and our professional power, so that we are being honest in our encounters with service users. Thus, we have to ask clear, direct and open questions. Nelson-Jones articulates this as simply asking the service user who is stuck with their resistant response, 'How is that behaviour helping you?' (2016: 98).

CASE STUDY 7.2

Hasraf and Omar are the maternal grandparents and carers to Jamil (14), who has cerebral palsy. They have strongly expressed a view to you (as a social worker from the children with disabilities team) that they do not need your support as they care for Jamil well. However, regulations state that this kinship care arrangement requires support and monitoring. How might you plan a way to engage Hasraf and Omar to work with you?

Achieving a balance between being a supportive and assertive practitioner is a continual challenge and requires constant self-reflection during which we examine our encounters. This allows us to reflect and consider any barriers to engagement, to establish whether the relationship is truly working or conversely if it is blocked. Woodcock Ross (2016) and Shulman (2016) use the term 'contracting' at the start of the working relationship: in essence this is an informal working agreement which recognises both parties have a valid point of view that should be respected. Shulman (2016) talks about the need for the worker to build a positive relationship, which involves generating feelings of rapport, trust and caring, of making people feel valued and cared about even when there are concerns about their behaviour. To help achieve and support this rapport as genuine, Shulman stresses the need for the worker to tap into painful emotions from their own life in order to be able to anticipate and to relate to some of the feelings service users may have at an affective level. Drawing on such feelings within ourselves enables us to better read a service user's behaviours such as shock or silence. It can also facilitate the ability to pace the conversation to give time and space to elicit emotional responses from the service user about how they truly feel. Drawing on your feelings and using empathy, showing that you recognise that your presence as a

TOURO COLLEGE LIBRARY

worker may be frightening or threatening, will allow you to offer suggestions to service users about how difficult this might be for them. Trotter (2006) provides a helpful reminder of the significance of power acting as a pressure on service users, who have often been labelled by society as flawed, as failing or as deviant. There is a genuine and strong sense of stigma that exists for involuntary service users, and living with such labels can cause individuals to have a poor sense of self and low self-esteem. An important part of the social worker role here is to be assertive enough to hold an open conversation which explores the hidden and difficult feelings of the service user, including listening to their perspective, worries and fears about working with you. Following on from this, you can begin to work on things that need to change by using goal setting strategies, and agreeing timescales together to review progress. During this 'working phase' of the relationship, if resistance is still a feature, and is halting or stalling the changes that are expected, it is important that the social worker does not ignore it. Avoiding this because it is difficult should not be attempted, as it can create a false sense that progress is taking place, when the reality is that practitioner and service user may have reached an impasse, an almost stalemate position. This false relationship embodies all the elements of resistance which can be illustrative of an underlying attempt by the service user to assert control over the working relationship.

REFLECTIVE TASK 7.3

Think of an example from a practice encounter, or a team/group work activity that you have been involved in, where the purpose of the work was stalling and people were avoiding talking about this.

- How did you react to this?
- What unhelpful behaviours can you identify in yourself and others that caused the stalling to persist?
- What helpful behaviours can you identify to get over avoidance?

In contemporary times, particularly following the inquiry into the tragic death of Peter Connelly (Laming, 2009), there has been increasing recognition of the role of disguised compliance (Munro, 2011), which frames this resistant behaviour using the language of collusion from service users. The messages from these reports highlight the importance of social workers acknowledging and being prepared to be more directive about resistance. They stress the importance of critical analysis of practice encounters to assist social workers to develop strategies to work with resistant service users. Shulman (2016) describes service users who are being reluctant and ambivalent towards doing what is required of them as lacking the ability to focus on the issues. He suggests that the worker's role is to ensure the conversation is steered towards 'holding this focus' (Shulman, 2016: 210). Therefore, it is important to explore ambivalent feelings and not to ignore them. Although it can be uncomfortable to raise issues, a common mistake that social workers make is to be overly positive and to believe that giving encouragement will overcome the difficulties. However, things will not change unless you take a different approach and address patterns of behaviour that are unhelpful.

CASE STUDY 7.2 CONTINUED

Reluctantly, Hasraf and Omar have engaged with you, and you now see them to offer support on a regular basis. Your assessment of Jamil's needs are that he needs to develop his independence as he approaches adulthood, as you assess that his carers 'baby' him. You talk to them, and they agree to develop his independence, but on future visits it is clear that they have not committed to it. Think of ways you could challenge this disguised compliance.

So far we have used the contracting framework to examine what is happening and why this might be the case. We have identified underlying messages about the importance of engaging in empathic ways to be able to reach a point in the encounter when the practitioner can begin to probe issues using a more assertive response. Writing within the discipline of business management, Shell (2006) provides an established and clear technique for negotiation skills that is helpful for social workers to include in their repertoire of interpersonal skills. This approach to problem solving identifies five patterns or styles of how we might address an encounter in which we are aiming to secure an agreed way forward. These styles are summarised below:

1. *Avoiding*: We may avoid the issue because we know it is painful and it will produce conflict. This is a useful technique to adopt when there is no great value placed on the outcome of the potential conflict, that is, it is not worth the argument. We may be able to see there is a place for this technique in problem solving in our interpersonal relationships. However, this is not applicable to social work practice where the stakes about interference into people's private spaces pose ethical issues.
2. *Accommodating*: This is illustrated by giving way and placating the other person at the expense of your own needs, with the intention of meeting the other person's needs. This is likely to occur within closer relationships that we value when one side does not want to damage the relationship. It is easy to recognise that this second style holds some parallels to what occurs in the middle phase of the working relationship between service user and practitioner. Here either party can find themselves accommodating their concerns and wishes in an attempt to hold onto the relationship. Additionally, this approach is also illustrative of the entrenched repetitive patterns that were discussed earlier in this chapter. If this is happening, the worker should use supervision to reflect on their own style, considering questions such as: Within

my role, am I being directive or authoritative with this person? Is our working agenda a shared one? How am I balancing the use of my professional and personal power in this relationship? Examining these questions closely with a supervisor will ensure principles of anti-discriminatory practice remain central to thinking and learning about yourself and your professional role.

3. *Compromising*: This usually occurs within valued established relationships and is an amalgamation of the previous two styles. A compromise is made to secure the middle ground between the two parties in order to move forward without huge dispute. Importantly, this does not have to follow legal principles of natural justice (Brammer, 2014) and fairness. This style of resolving interpersonal conflicts can be seen within professional working relationships, perhaps best illustrated within team dynamics and creative professional sharing of perspectives.

4. *Collaborating*: Within a practitioner and service users relationship the fourth style, collaborating, is perhaps the closest to traditional aspects of person-centred practice (Gibson, 2014). This is because it strives to achieve solutions based on both parties' goals in an overall approach that aims to recognise that each side has a valuable contribution to make. It is a style towards negotiation that works well when the problem at stake is of value to both sides. Therefore, it is useful when clarifying what is significant and what the next steps should be.

5. *Competing*: This is more applicable to the capitalist context of a business market, where the stakes are high and based on wins and losses at the cost of fairness and the impact on others. This style is characterised as an aggressive state which drives the competition forwards. Clearly there is no direct link between this approach and direct work with service users in a social care setting. However, Shell's framework is applicable to help the practitioner to reflect holistically on their own default style towards problem solving within interpersonal and professional relationships. The practitioner can also share this knowledge and insight with service users who struggle to express their wishes in a collaborative way, thus assisting them to develop and improve their interpersonal skills for more successful outcomes.

CASE STUDY 7.2 CONTINUED

In the case of kinship carers Hasraf and Omar, consider how you will approach planning to raise your concerns with this family. Using Shell's negotiation skills, which style of problem solving do you think you naturally assume and why?

COMMUNICATION SKILLS AUDIT: WORKING WITH RESISTANCE

Finally, reflect on your strengths and areas for development in relation to working with resistance and identify two or three action points for you to develop (Table 7.1).

Table 7.1   Communication skills audit: working with resistance

	Strengths in recognising resistant behaviours	Areas for development	Action points to improve your ability to work with resistant behaviours
Domain 1 Professionalism			
Domain 3 Diversity			
Domain 4 Rights and justice			
Domain 6 Critical reflection and analysis			
Domain 7 Intervention and skills			

CONCLUSION

This chapter has explored some of the dynamics of resistance and reluctant behaviours that can be a common feature in service user and social work encounters. A body of knowledge from a counselling perspective offers an important framework to assist this exploration of what is happening psychologically for service users at times of high stress, when they begin working with a social worker or reach a stage when change is explicitly expected by professionals. Strategies to critically reflect on your own default style of both coping with resistant behaviour and negotiating through such encounters have been discussed as a template for practice. The literature confirms the importance of the need for social work practitioners to be clear about their purpose and work within the authority of their role with a skilful, transparent and assertively respectful demeanour. We can practice and learn over time these valuable qualities, beginning with good-quality supervision in initial training and ongoing critically reflexive practice.

FURTHER READING

Gast, L. and Bailey, M. (2014) *Mastering Communication in Social Work*. London: Jessica Kingsley. Chapter Four, 'Communication where there is resistance or reluctance', provides insight into types of and reasons for resistance and how to address them.

Rogers, M., Whitaker, D., Edmondson, D. and Peach, D. (2016) *Developing Skills for Social Work Practice*. London: Sage. Chapter Fourteen, 'Conflict management and resolution', encourages the reader to reflect on self-awareness within conflict resolution.

BARRIERS TO EFFECTIVE COMMUNICATION

Links to Knowledge and Skills Statements

Adults: person-centred practice; effective assessments and outcome-based support planning; direct work with individuals and families; supervision, critical reflection and analysis; organisational context; professional ethics and leadership

Children's: relationships and effective direct work; communication; child and family assessment; analysis, decision making, planning and review; role of supervision; organisational context

INTRODUCTION

This chapter will critically analyse the factors that prevent positive communication. This book is primarily focused on what you can do: a strengths-based perspective on developing your communication skills. This chapter, however, focuses more on what you should not do. Following on from the chapters thus far, it will consider the issues that might restrict your ability to engage, listen, empathise, clarify and challenge. It will also reflect on the barriers to good written communication, multi-agency communication and endings. It is designed to stimulate you to reflect on whether any of the issues discussed are impeding your work on a long- or short-term basis.

ACTIVITY 8.1

Make a list of your less favourable personality traits.

If this is a hard activity for you, immediately refer back to Chapter One on emotional intelligence and reflection to develop your self-awareness further. However, most of us are acutely aware of our areas to develop by this point in the book. This exercise is not meant to crush your self-confidence and highlight your faults. Rather it is meant to develop your thinking as you progress through this chapter in terms of: 'Is this an area that I need to develop?' For instance, you may be opinionated, and when communicating with service users, have to ensure to remember not to express opinions just because you can (and want to), but to listen to their opinions. However, this might also mean that in multi-agency meetings you are assertive and able to advocate for the service user confidently. In other words, areas to develop in one situation can be your strengths in other areas. It is about developing appropriate responses to the individual circumstance. We will now reflect on the issues that can impact on us as communicators. But remember, there will be days when a service user just does not want to communicate, and a positive assessment to rearrange is called for if it is viable.

BARRIERS TO EFFECTIVE INITIAL ENGAGEMENT

Power

However powerless you may feel as a social work student, it can be guaranteed that your service user will feel even more powerless. The reality is that they still see you as the agent of decision-making and control. Remember that your presentation can state that you have power, from wearing a suit to eye contact: non-verbal communication can communicate power or partnership. It is likely that the service user has been oppressed by society: perhaps because of socially constructed negative connotations associated with their service user group, for example alcohol misusing mothers seen as unloving and selfish: or the perceived limited contributions to society of adults with a learning disability; or because the group with whom the service user identifies have been excluded from services and decision making, leaving them powerless and oppressed (see Chapter Four). Thompson (2015a) argues that in order to avoid being a further oppressive force in the service user's life, you should empower the service user and enable them to make informed decisions, avoiding patronising terminology and seeing the strengths of the service user by working in partnership with them. Yet there will be times when power is both legitimate and necessary. As a social worker, you will have to operate within powerful situations to assert control and safeguard children and adults. There is a fine line for a student social worker to tread between assertive use of appropriate power and the wielding of power, which comes with practice and experience.

Oppressive practice

Much is written about anti-discriminatory practice and anti-oppressive practice, and it is not the intention of this short section to attempt to dissect the issues involved. However, as a student social worker, a clear barrier to your engagement with a service user is to be oppressive to them as an individual. For example, Baum (2017) asserts that fathers have traditionally been consulted less, so therefore their wishes and feelings have been marginalised at the expense of the parenting mother. She argues that awareness of power differentials (both yours as the social worker and theirs as a male) must be acknowledged and addressed to engage the father and avoid oppressive practice.

As a student social worker, you will work with service users from a multitude of ethnic backgrounds; of a different age, class or gender than your own; and who have experienced things that you never will. In order to ensure that this does not hinder your initial (and subsequent) engagement with the service user, you will need to be mindful of the differences. This is not to say that you should walk in and state the obvious differences from the outset, but that you should be aware of them and the impact that they can have on your relationship.

As a student social worker, you will benefit from being aware of the characteristics and customs of different cultures, whilst not assuming that this will be the case with all service users. Egan (2014) reminds us that we can have *blind spots*, where we assume that because a person has a certain background they will behave in a certain way. For example, to assume that an older Asian Muslim gentleman will not accept the support of a younger White woman would be to pre-empt failure, and more than likely guarantee it. It would be as big a mistake to assume that because a Black African woman verbally agreed with you as a student social worker, she did not really agree with you but was faithful to her cultural upbringing of respecting figures of power, just as it would be to assume that she was compliant. Egan (2014) recommends an awareness of cultural and diversity issues, whilst approaching each service user as an individual and not as a 'collective'. The most important thing to remember is *not to assume*, but to communicate with the service user as an individual, whilst remaining aware of cultural norms that may be indicators.

However, remember that the agency procedures you work within can steer you towards oppressive practice. A local authority that is risk-averse following a series of tragedies and removes children with low thresholds of risk will have a different philosophy (but one could argue equally oppressive) from one that has no funds and is unable to provide much needed services. Whilst it is your responsibility as an employee of that agency to follow their philosophy and implement their procedures, it is also your responsibility to advocate against oppressive practice.

Repetitive, set responses

The social worker who tells you that they communicate well with the service user utilising their, for example, light-hearted initial engagement skills on every occasion is a complacent social worker who is likely to lose insight and motivation. Once a social worker feels confident and comfortable with one way of communicating it can be easy to fall into the trap of using this method that is effective and therefore needs no further thought or development. The social worker may become stale, make assumptions, and be less likely to respond to the service user's individual needs. Think about the conscious competence matrix in Chapter One. It is likely that this social worker varies between unconscious competence and unconscious incompetence, depending on the service user's individual response. Horwath (2016) reminds us that in order to maximise the service user's commitment, the social worker needs also to be committed.

The philosophy of a person-centred approach is that each service user is an individual, with individual needs, wishes and feelings, which you, as the student social worker, should hear and respond to: to pretend that there is one way to communicate with all service users is both naïve and inflexible. Thompson (2015a) reflects on the need for social work responses to be creative and flexible, which benefits both the student social worker (as they avoid stagnation) and the service user (as they receive a more individual service). Each student social worker should develop a social work tool-belt, akin to a builder's tool-belt, where you develop understanding and skills in a wide range of interventions and theories and draw on the right tool for the right job. Naturally there will be some tools (or communication styles) that you utilise more often as they are well suited to your personality and style of social work, but you will need to vary this to respond to the needs of different service users. It is *your* responsibility to adjust your communication style to best meet the situation and produce a positive outcome.

Problem solving

Many prospective social work students cite that they want to help people as their motivation to become social workers. However, communication is not about resolving problems, but about listening to service users' wishes and feelings and working in partnership with them to mutually agree person-centred solutions. A barrier to engaging can be when you are so busy trying to help that you forget to listen to what the service user wants help with.

BARRIERS TO EFFECTIVE LISTENING

Physical conditions

The physical conditions of the place where you will communicate will impact on your ability to do so effectively. Consider your own needs versus the service user's rights and feelings. A fear of dogs raises the ethical dilemma of risking offending the service user, but terror can be a disabling feeling, leaving you unable to listen and therefore communicate effectively. What if you cannot hear the service user due to a loud television or stereo? Will you ask them to turn it down? Every social worker will, half in humour, half in embarrassment of their judgement, tell you about the 'sofa hover', where you test all your core strength to sit just above a wet sofa, or the room that had no furniture so they had to crouch on the floor. We are expected to communicate within a variety of home conditions, and do this without judgement, or else our judgement may cloud our ability to hear the service user.

Over-eagerness or anxiety about performance

If you are distracted from your role as a listener, you are less likely to listen effectively. With practice the skilled student social worker will develop confidence in their listening skills, and be able to hear more. As with all skills, 'practise makes perfect' – the more you practise with family and friends, and subsequently service users, the more confident you will be, and the more you will be able to relax into the role. Furthermore, Whittaker and Havard (2016) explore the development of defensive practices, that is, student social workers prioritising being seen to do the right thing rather than actually listening to the service user's wishes and feelings and needs.

Stress levels

It is inevitable as a student social worker that you will have times when you have one more case than is viable to manage, and/or that you will have busier periods on your caseload. It is important that when you go into an interview with a service user to leave that outside for a short while and concentrate on the moment. If you are stressed, your performance as a student social worker will likely deteriorate. As a student social worker, you will need to identify when you are becoming stressed and develop coping strategies to deal with stress, not least gaining supervisor support. As discussed in Chapter One, self-awareness and emotional intelligence are necessary to avoid distraction.

Differences in agenda

Many times when meeting a service user, the student social worker will attend with an agenda: assess the situation, close the case or inform the service user of an outcome. It is not unusual for the service user to have a different agenda: their argument with their sister yesterday, their lack of housing benefit, memories of their beloved husband. The student social worker must develop the skill of allowing the service user to be heard and valued whilst also addressing their often procedural agenda. This means balancing between listening and empathy and assertiveness.

Conflict

If you become involved in a conflict situation with a service user, you may find it difficult to listen to them effectively, particularly if you feel you are at risk or if you become angry as a response to the conflict. Remember that even in a conflict situation, respecting the service user by listening empathetically to their perspective will engage him/her.

Note taking

Koprowska (2014) recognises that taking notes can detract from your observational assessment and lack of eye contact can disengage a service user as you present as too procedural. However, she also recognises that without notes, you may not remember crucial details. We advise developing a style of note taking where words can stimulate memory of discussion and important facts are always noted. But most importantly, writing up of notes immediately after an intervention will ensure optimum recall.

BARRIERS TO EFFECTIVE CLARIFICATION

Sometimes, as a student social worker you will need to provide the service user with information, so that they can make an informed decision that will impact on their life. You will need to be clear and accurate.

REFLECTIVE TASK 8.1

You are visiting a service user's house and they ask about service options in relation to their child with a disability. You are a child protection student social worker, and do not have that knowledge. How do you respond?

It may be tempting in a panic to 'make something up'. It is imperative that you do not give the service user wrong information. Not only will it mean that they are unable to make an informed decision, but if they no longer feel that they can trust you, they will disengage from the working relationship. In our experience, simply stating that you do not know but will find out and come back to them within a week with the information (and do so) engages service users with both your honesty and integrity, and your reliability. Thompson (2015a) reminds us to avoid vague and ambiguous information, and to be clear in what we are saying. Mantell (2013) reminds us that when working with a number of family members, or agencies with conflicting perspectives and needs, you will need to be very clear in your role, to avoid confusion.

Clarification, as discussed in Chapter Four, is also about reviewing the information and discussion to ensure that the service user has understood what you have said, not just assume that they have. It would be condescending to ask the service user to repeat what you have just agreed to clarify that they understood, but neither can you expect them to be empowered to ask for further details. Furthermore, Mantell (2013) highlights that dissonance can develop between the social worker's and service user's perspective if the student social worker assumes that the service user remains fixed in their position, forgetting that our intervention can, and should, impact on their needs and wishes and feelings. He recommends the use of ongoing clarification, often through simple review, to avoid this happening.

BARRIERS TO EFFECTIVE EMPATHY

Judgemental approach

The mantra for any student social worker should be to communicate in a non-judgemental manner. However, it must be recognised that this can be difficult to achieve all the time. When trying to be empathic, the student social worker needs to hear the service user's perspective, but if the student social worker has made a judgemental assumption about the service user, they may find it hard to listen to the service user and be empathic. Egan (2014) reminds us not to see the service user as a victim or fragile. If you are coming from a perspective that the service user is incapable, you will not hear that they have strengths, and your responses will lack empathy. Similarly, Egan (2014) reminds us that if we make assumptions about a service user's ability or inability based on their appearance, we may limit our ability to hear their perspective.

REFLECTIVE TASK 8.2

Michael presents at the duty office. He is in his mid-forties and appears unkempt and a little aggressive. Answer honestly: what is your assumption about the reason for his visit?

Would you be surprised to hear that Michael is a service user's drug worker (no offence to drug workers) and is cross because he is attending the office for the fourth cancelled appointment with your colleague? If you approach him with a judgemental attitude, you might alienate him further and the service user's needs will be less likely to be met. Grant and Brewer (2014) argue that poor reflection, from a personal or a procedural perspective, can lead to a lack of empathy. By reflecting on one's judgemental assumptions, the student social worker can recognise and counter them, leaving you open to listening to and empathising with the service user's perspective.

Negative social work

There is nothing worse than arriving at a service user's house and telling them that nothing can be done.

REFLECTIVE TASK 8.3

Imagine you are looking to sell your house or rent a property and the estate agent tells you that it is impossible. How does that feel?

It is likely that you will feel demotivated, and less likely to try to resolve your housing issue. However, if the estate agent appears cheerful, you will be more committed to their services. It is imperative as student social workers that we present a strengths-based perspective with all interventions. Constable (2013) argues that if you are a naturally pessimistic person, you can practise positive responses and change your approach to a more positive one. This way you are not condemning the service user before they begin. She argues that self-awareness of your negativity is necessary before you can effect change, which requires an element of emotional intelligence. Thompson (2015a) reminds us that being negative about an outcome can be as unbalanced as being positive. He argues that as a student social worker you should be *realistic*, that is, optimistic of a positive outcome whilst not blinded to concerns.

Poor responses

Egan (2014) recommends that the following styles of response are best avoided as they lack empathy:

- No response
- Distracting questions
- Clichés
- Interpretations
- Advice

- Parroting
- Agreement and sympathy
- Faking it

By utilising the positive communication skills that are suggested throughout this book, you will learn to avoid these responses.

Use of *self*

There is much debate about the ethics of using your own experiences in communicating with a service user. On the one hand, there is the philosophy that in order to remain professional, one has to remain aloof: share nothing of your own experiences with the service user lest they see you as vulnerable, or as a friend. On the other hand, there is the philosophy that by sharing your experiences you will model positive responses (Egan, 2014) that the service user can reflect on and adopt as coping strategies. It is considered best to be mindful of both the nature and frequency of doing so. Relationship-based social work aims to use only enough of self to ensure that the service user's perspective takes priority and you do not forget to hear and understand their perspective.

Student social workers have a life too, and you may have experienced similar personal situations that you now face professionally. This can result in too much empathy becoming sympathy, or too harsh a reaction, each resulting in a subjective response to the service user based on your own feelings. It is critical that the student social worker does not over-identify with the service user's issues, as this can lead to projection of feelings.

Mantell (2013) argues that you cannot avoid using the self in communication, as your identity immediately engages or disengages the service user. He argues that your gender, culture, age, appearance, etc. are a part of your *self* that impacts on your communication; that your personality comes through in your preferred communication style; and that your non-verbal habits often communicate your strengths and weaknesses. Many of these will be subconscious communications, for example the student social worker who twiddles their hair when she is anxious. As you progress in the placement, observations of yourself will help you to identify these *self* communications.

BARRIERS TO EFFECTIVE CHALLENGING

Confidence/assertiveness

Thompson (2015a) reflects on the importance of being assertive, which he argues should be neither aggressive nor submissive. A student social worker who challenges aggressively will alienate the service user, and be unlikely to empower change, whilst a submissive student social worker fails to stimulate change by their lack of support. Egan (2014) believes that challenging too quickly is worse than being reluctant to challenge. As a student social worker, you will need to assess when challenge is necessary, where and when it is most effective, and how to do it in the most sensitive yet clear manner.

If you know that your personality is extreme in either direction, for example bossy or meek, you will need to develop a more confident, assertive manner (see Chapter Six). But remember, quiet is not submissive. Some of the best student social workers that we have known have been quietly assertive.

ACTIVITY 8.2

Practise assertive responses to the following scenarios:

- In a group activity at university, a peer is not undertaking their agreed tasks.
- At placement, you are asked to undertake a lone visit without a risk-assessment in place.
- Your cohort asks you to represent a concern to your course leader.

Activity 8.2 will aid your communication skills audit at the end of the chapter, as it will assist you to identify your strengths and areas for development.

Thompson (2015a) reminds us that assertiveness can be gender, class and culturally differently perceived, the implication being that if you are a White middle-class male student, you would have been raised to be assertive. Constable (2013) notes that a student social worker may wish to avoid conflict, so they may be less assertive or may be over-confident and present as aggressive. This may be because of personality, learnt behaviours or burn out. She argues that an unconfident, apologetic or vague approach can leave the service user unclear, and an aggressive, over-confident student social worker can lead the service user to disengage. It is important to be aware of both your personality and the identity perspective. Once again, your emotional intelligence will need to be utilised so that you can recognise your strengths and areas for development to become assertive.

Games

Thompson (2015a) also reminds us that people play *games*, and that the student social worker must be wary not to collude or to compete. This can be because of the service user feeling threatened, for example by a powerfully perceived social worker, or because it is the service user's coping strategy or normal behaviour.

CASE STUDY 8.1

Hazel and Rick have four children whose names are on the Child Protection Register due to parental domestic abuse and drug use. Hazel reports further domestic abuse to the student social worker, who takes her male manager to visit the couple to discuss the concerns.
Consider these three responses. Can you identify the game being played?

- Rick engages the manager immediately and makes jokey, sexist remarks about women. Hazel is not allowed to talk. The manager leaves reassured that there are no risks to the children.
- Rick confronts the manager immediately and aggressively. When the manager asks questions, Rick responds angrily and blames the system. The manager spends time on an ethical debate and discussion on the merits of the system and leaves with no further clarity.
- Rick confronts the manager immediately and aggressively. The manager reacts with anger, and a power battle ensues in which neither man is prepared to negotiate or compromise. The manager leaves and decides to escalate the concerns.

In each of the scenarios, Rick is avoiding discussing the domestic abuse and is manipulating the situation. In the first scenario, he draws the manager in to collude with him through identifying their similarities, and in the second he deflects discussion of the concerns, thus manipulating both situations. In the third example, the game is one of which male is the most powerful, often referred to as the alpha male. Not every 'game player' is aware that they are playing the game. It may be a deeply entrenched behaviour, within the constraints of which you will have to work. The important thing is to be aware of the possibilities but not obsess that they will happen, or you will trust no-one.

Also remember the challenge of disguised compliance: where a service user will state that they will work with you, but do not evidence any action that they have.

BARRIERS TO EFFECTIVE WRITTEN COMMUNICATION

Misunderstandings

Consider how written language can be misinterpreted.

REFLECTIVE TASK 8.4

You receive an email from your manager: Can I see you tomorrow for a quick chat?

Does this delight you or fill you with dread?

The issue here is that a lack of non-verbal communication, which we discussed above, means there is no point of reference as to whether this is a threat or a treat. Written communication is often a briefer communication and contains none of the detail to clarify meaning. From a service user's perspective, sometimes written communication can ensure that they *hear* what is said, as when it is in ink it is hard to avoid. However, it is also open to reading from one's own perspective. So, when utilising written communication to express something, ensure that it is clear and not open to interpretation. Furthermore, Francis et al. (2015) argue that our workload and the tone of the initial email will influence our interpretation of the communication, and therefore determine the tone with which we respond. Whilst we cannot influence stress levels, we can ensure that we send what Francis and colleagues term as *civil* emails and err on the side of positivity when reading emails.

Thought will need to be given to the appropriateness of written communication if the service user's first language is not English. You can use online translation tools to enable translation but be aware that they can also mistranslate. A variety of IT software will read out electronic communication for the receiver if they have literacy difficulties. But remember that they may need support accessing such technology or just not be interested. Borg et al. (2015) reviewed international research on advice on supporting people with a 'cognitive disability' to communicate electronically, and found that the support and settings (for example, text size, screen colour) that they needed depended on their disability and individual needs. Needless to say, to support a service user, exploring their individual needs from a person-centred perspective will enhance their ability to communicate with you.

BARRIERS TO EFFECTIVE INTER-PROFESSIONAL COMMUNICATION

In the multi-disciplinary context, a range of factors may, in some circumstances, affect how professionals communicate.

Familiarity

This includes any past history of contact, directly or indirectly experienced. Whilst you can have a positive impression of a service or individual professional, a previous personal or reported poor working relationship can create a negative first impression, and restrict your openness, which will in turn lead to poor practice.

If your contact with the service is on a frequent basis, then you are likely to understand the service provision criteria. But remember that criteria can be very specific and can change, which can be frustrating.

Different remits

There can be confusion and dissonant expectations the first time when working with a service. Different services can come from different perspectives, for example the social and medical models of practice. However, they should complement and not compete with each other if you communicate well with each other.

Organisational and other constraints may affect how well professionals can listen to each other. Some busy teams may have to have a stringent system of prioritisation. The person you are trying to refer may not meet the threshold for involvement and this may make you feel like your concerns are not being listened to. You may be offered signposting instead or suggestions about other services, perhaps provided by the voluntary or independent sector. Also think about our discussions earlier in this chapter about the impact on your presentation when you have a high workload: this will apply to other professionals too.

Method of contact

Professionals often communicate through indirect means, such as email and telephone, and Chapter Nine discusses this aspect in more detail. But do not rely on these communications as an alternative to face-to-face contact, as indirect contact can lead to a lack of engagement with the process and limit the sharing of information. Indirect contact should be supplemented with formal and informal meetings to make decisions with both the professionals and service user involved.

Information sharing issues

Working Together (Department for Education, 2015) clearly states that information should be shared that could enable decisions to be made that can support a child at risk of significant harm. This is a philosophy that is shared across children's and adults' service provision. However, it does not always happen. This can be because of fear of sharing or where it will lead to on a personal or organisational level. Or it can be because of procedures that prevent professionals from sharing information or oversight by an overworked professional. If you take the perspective that you need to update yourself with information from all those involved in supporting a service user through open and honest communication, you will minimise such problems occurring.

However frustrated you are with another professional's communication, look at your own communication and relationship with them, and check if you are opening or closing the communication channels.

BARRIERS TO EFFECTIVE ENDINGS

Dependency

When a student social worker does a good job, they should do themselves out of a job! Your aim should be to empower the service user to resolve future difficulties with the skills and confidence that they have developed with your support. However, it is often not that simple. Service users might see that you have been a positive support and become reliant on you to continue to empower and positively reinforce their skills. Whilst press reports may not make you believe this, service users can come to see you as a friend, part of their support network, and become dependent on your visits. This can make ending an intervention emotionally difficult both for you and the service user. As discussed in Chapter Twelve, you will need to plan the ending, and provide explanation and notice to support the service user through this necessary process. Thompson (2015a) reminds us that people often dislike change, in particular when they feel comfortable with an arrangement. He recommends that as a student social worker you review the positive achievements made in your work together with the service user and identify other support networks so that a void is not left with your withdrawal.

Procedural pressures

It can be frustrating for a student social worker when their work is called to an end due to procedural perspectives. This may be because the service user has reached the end of the maximum allocation, or that criteria have changed and they are no longer eligible. As the student social worker, it is your duty not only to advocate the service user's needs, but also to respect and adhere to the agency's procedure. This may make creating a positive ending more difficult to facilitate, but it will be your duty to present a positive slant, irrespective of your personal opinion.

 COMMUNICATION SKILLS AUDIT: BARRIERS TO EFFECTIVE COMMUNICATION SKILLS

Finally, reflect on your areas for development in relation to the barriers that may impede your communication and identify two or three action points for you to develop (Table 8.1).

Table 8.1   Communication skills audit: barriers to effective communication skills

	Strengths in communication skills	Areas for development	Action points to improve communication skills
Domain 1 Professionalism			
Domain 3 Diversity			
Domain 6 Critical reflection and analysis			
Domain 8 Contexts and organisations			

CONCLUSION

This chapter has asked you to reflect on the factors that might prevent good communication. Some of these issues are transient, and location and time specific, some are more personal. For each of them, you will need to reflect on how they impact on *you*, and develop coping strategies to minimise their impact on your relationship with your service user. Being aware of the issues that may limit your communication is part of your emotional intelligence, so that you can address them and enhance your communication.

Finally, Egan (2014) reminds us that communication is but one skill that we need to use. If we become so entrenched in talking that we forget to intervene, then our communication is valueless. He reminds us that our communication should be flexible to our individual service user's needs, and that we should continually develop our communication skills through ongoing training and practice.

FURTHER READING

Egan, G. (2014) *The Skilled Helper: A Client-certred Approach*, 10th edn. Hampshire: Cengage Learning.
Mantell, A. (ed.) (2013) *Skills for Social Work Practice*. London: Sage.
Thompson, N. (2015) *People Skills*. Basingstoke, Hampshire: Palgrave Macmillan.

All three books address the barriers that a social worker will face in all forms of communication, making them good sources of information and advice.

WRITTEN COMMUNICATION: CASE RECORDING, LETTERS, TEXTS, SOCIAL MEDIA

Links to Knowledge and Skills Statements

Adults: role of social workers working with adults; person-centred practice; effective assessments and outcome-based support planning; direct work with individuals and families; supervision, critical reflection and analysis; organisational context; professional ethics and leadership

Children's: relationships and effective direct work; communication; child and family assessment; analysis, decision making, planning and review; role of supervision; organisational context

INTRODUCTION

This chapter will ask the reader to reflect on the importance of prompt and appropriate recording, and put this into a procedural context. Examples of poor written case recordings will be provided to ask the reader to reflect on their content and how they could be enhanced, and they will be asked to rewrite the recordings for their development.

This chapter will also reflect on the different styles of communication necessary when utilising written communication, including text, letters and social media. It will offer the student direction on effective writing, and ask them to reflect on their written skills audit. The quality of your written work will be assessed when you are on a social work placement and contribute to your practice educator's assessment of your professionalism (Domain 1) and ability to intervene (Domain 7).

Frith and Martin (2015) recommend that before you start to write in a professional context you should first understand its purpose. This will enable you to determine the information the written piece needs to impart, its audience, and the style to adopt. Most social work offices have proformas for all occasions, so be sure to inform yourself of them. For us, the most important aspect of any writing is that it is clear and concise. The reader must be able to get to the necessary information effectively.

CASE RECORDING

Case recording is an essential social work task. The Health and Care Professions Council document *Standards of Conduct, Performance and Ethics* recognises this importance and Section 10 states:

10 Keep records of your work

Keep accurate records

10.1 You must keep full, clear, and accurate records for everyone you care for, treat, or provide other services to.

10.2 You must complete all records promptly and as soon as possible after providing care, treatment or other services.

Keep records secure

10.3 You must keep records secure by protecting them from loss, damage or inappropriate access. (HCPC, 2016b: 10)

There is a saying 'If it isn't written down, it didn't happen', and this is never truer than in social work. The written work should be given as equal importance as the home visit or the multi-agency meeting. A good student social worker schedules daily or (at worst) weekly time into their schedule to complete case recordings. In this way all notes are made contemporaneously and they reflect the current recollection of events, not recollections that are influenced by subsequent events.

ACTIVITY 9.1

Write a brief, factual account of your first day on your social work course. Think about who you talked to and where you went. What was the lecture?
  Now stop for a minute and ask yourself several questions:

- How accurate is the account? Has the gap between then and now (several weeks, months or even years) impacted on the clarity of your memory?
- How do you see the day? Has your perception of it changed as you have made friends/got to know your way round/experienced other lectures?

A good recording is made on the day of the event, so that you have a clear, objective perspective of the event. Each agency, statutory or voluntary, will have a policy on recording, often that it should be completed within 24 hours. It is imperative that you both know, and adhere to, the policy.

WHY DO WE RECORD?

A good case record is one which is focused and evidenced based, and provides the primary audience with information they can use to gain a good sense of the situation and make good recommendations for future action. (Healy and Mulholland, 2012: 69)

The overriding issue is that of providing the agency with a clear case management history. Healy and Mulholland (2012) refer to this as the *primary audience*. By recording everything on a service user's case notes, even unanswered telephone calls, you record both your actions and the service user's. This will enable clear evidence-based decision making that is able to safeguard the service user and meet their needs effectively. For example, attending a resource panel to argue for services for a young person with a physical disability will require a clear summary of his needs, previous support provided and its outcome. The case notes will enable you to gather the information and provide clear communication to the panel. You will be more confident of your ability to advocate on the service user's behalf if you have clear case recording, that is, so that you have the facts that support your argument. O'Rourke (2010) discusses the need for clear case recording to support decision making, calling it a *crucial information base*, but also reflects that all recording is *surveillance*, as it leaves a record of all events. She reflects on the impact of this structural power differential, and reminds the student social worker to be vigilant and sensitive to such issues.

REFLECTIVE TASK 9.1

Imagine you are the duty student social worker. Alf arrives at the office and states that his social worker, who he says is off for the week, promised he could collect £20 section 17 (child in need) money for his daughter's uniform as she starts school next week.

You take two actions. Firstly, you need to review the case recording, as the social worker should have left a clear record that this would happen. Secondly, you ask the manager if this has been agreed. Unfortunately, there are no recordings on the case file for the last month, and the manager is not available. You have no way of knowing if Alf has this agreement in place or not and are unable to provide the money. Alf becomes verbally aggressive, and whilst you are able to utilise your empathy skills, and communicate clearly with him, you are unable to resolve this issue for him.

How do you feel?

It is likely that you will feel frustrated that your job was difficult because you did not have the information that you needed to undertake a simple task. Whilst this is a simple example of the need for clear recording to enable decisions, it is how social work decisions are made: by reviewing previous decisions and interventions, appropriate informed decisions can be made.

Often decisions related to service users will be made based on recorded patterns of behaviour, evidence of successful or unsuccessful interventions, and information from multi-agency information sharing. Whilst the next chapter will refer to chronologies in more detail, these decision-making tools can only be formulated with clear accurate information from the case records. O'Rourke (2010) raises a word of caution here: student social workers may face the ethical decision of writing notes from a risk perspective, to ensure that their service user meets the eligibility criteria. However, this approach contradicts the person-centred and strengths-based or restorative perspective within which they work with the service user.

Furthermore, those decisions that are based on your case notes should also become case records. All management decisions should be recorded on your service user's files to show when and how decisions were made. Whilst recognising that case recording had become overly bureaucratic at the expense of quality creative and flexible social work, Munro still asserted that 'recording is a key social work task and its centrality to the protection of children cannot be overestimated' (2011: 114).

There is of course also the bleaker side of case recording, that of accountability: showing that you have done your job as you ought. Sadly, in modern society there is a blame culture, whereby if a tragedy occurs, your work will be scrutinised and someone will be found to be at fault. Following the death of a service user, there will be a serious case review, which will review the case recordings that cannot be added to if you realise that you had forgotten to write in information. Of course, serious case reviews also highlight institutional poor practice, and often improve practice for the better. For example, the East Riding (2013) serious case review of the death of a young person recommended that the existing policy on recording within clear timeframes should be emphasised by the agency. This highlights that sometimes recording can be seen by teams and agencies as a lower priority, with a socially constructed philosophy of interventions being more important. The prioritisation of case recording is not only your responsibility but also the team manager's responsibility to foster a philosophy of prioritising the recording of work undertaken. This should not just be seen as the recording of the important, monitored interventions, such as visits to looked-after children within specified timescales to meet Ofsted demands, but all aspects of work undertaken.

Another thought that you should have when writing your case recordings is: the service user will see my case recording if they ask for access to their records, and whom Healy and Mulholland (2012) refer to as the *secondary audience*. Whilst this is not a service user-centred approach, it is, pragmatically, a realistic one in today's recording procedure. The philosophy that student social workers should proactively share their notes with the service user about whom they are writing is a very person-centred approach to case recording. This approach helps the student social worker to focus on case recording that is well written and adheres to the principles discussed below. However, this proactive philosophy is relatively rare in social work.

REFLECTIVE TASK 9.2

You undertake a visit to your doctor and you feel strongly that they perceived you as a time waster. You then observe her writing notes about you. These notes will influence how other doctors see you on future visits. Would you like to see the notes about you?

It's an ethical dilemma, isn't it? We should trust the professionalism of our medical expert, but there is also that personal concern about how we may have been represented. Now, imagine that you are a service user, with judgements being made about you by professionals all the time. Decisions are being made about you based on these recordings, possibly even the removal of your children. Many service users will decide that they want to see what is written about them, and that is their legal right. Under the Data Protection Act 1998 they can ask to see their case notes (excluding those relating to other people) at any time they wish to do so. This may be whilst you are working with them or some time afterwards. An adult may read historical records of their time in foster or residential care to help them to develop their understanding of decisions made and their identity. Murray and Humphreys (2014) note that incomplete or value-laden case records restricted closure. Consequently, it is important that you write your case notes as though the service user will see them at some point in the future, which means writing them from an objective and factual perspective in a clear manner.

O'Rourke (2010) reminds us that the student social worker will experience a perennial ethical battle between advocating for the service user and representing the agency, but that both perspectives should be equally important. Her research concluded that most case recording is never seen, making recording a frustrating task, but when it is looked at, it is imperative that it is undertaken well.

COMMUNICATION SKILLS FOR CASE RECORDING

Ensure that you are clear in your content and context

It is critical that when recording you are clear. A duty or reallocated social worker, who will not have your understanding and contextual knowledge, should be able to review your case recording and be able to see clearly what happened. The case recording should include when and where an intervention happened and whom it included. It should include what was discussed, any areas of contention (noting both perspectives), actions agreed and outcomes.

Be concise

By reading a clear, concise record of an intervention the reader will be able to identify what happened and what was agreed. If you have a tendency to write reams when you could write it more concisely, you will need to practise this skill. As an additional advantage, it will enhance your assignment writing skills too.

Write well

You should also practise good grammatical writing, with awareness of spelling. Frith and Martin (2015) provide an excellent overview of grammatical rules. With today's dependence on computer records, all spellings and grammar should be checked electronically, but not all mistakes are recognised by the spell-checker. The difference in recording that states that a mother is *not* (instead of *now*) drug free is significant. You should avoid the use of acronyms, even where you feel they are obvious. Just because you understand one, does not mean future readers will. If you know that written English is not your strength, utilise support whilst you are in university to develop these skills. They are a basic social work expectation.

Describe relevant detail

Deciding what to include and what to leave out is always a difficult decision. You could argue that the weather is never relevant, but if it is icy cold and the service user's child is wearing only a nappy in the garden, it would be relevant to record. As a rule of thumb, record concerns and improvements, record difference between visits, and record the service user's perspective. Look at the case recording in Activity 9.2 later in the chapter: are there areas that you feel are more or less relevant for the case recording?

Strengths-based perspective

Constable (2013) reflects that, as with many social work verbal communications, case recordings should be written from a strengths-based perspective. She argues focusing on the positives achieved rather than the negatives. The next chapter will return to strengths-based perspective writing.

Be respectful of your client

When writing case records, you need to think of how you refer to the service user. If you bear in mind that potentially they will read your case records, this should guide you as to how to write about them. Ensure that your case records are non-judgemental and are sensitive to the service user, no matter how grave the concerns. As a student social worker you will have a significant level of structural power, and whilst that cannot be eradicated, it can be reduced by ensuring that you work with the service user by valuing them as an individual and respecting their rights. The *Standards of Conduct, Performance and Ethics* first standard requires the student social worker to work with the service user by 'respecting their privacy and dignity ... [and] ... work in partnership' (HCPC, 2016b: 5). This can only be achieved if the student social worker utilises respectful recording techniques.

Reporting another's speech and opinion

Case recording does not require a verbatim copy of the entire conversation, instead a summary of the conversation should be provided. Ensure that the service user/ professional's perspective is included in an objective impartial manner. Utilise the skills discussed in the summarising section in Chapter Four to write a clear concise summary of the conversation. Occasionally a direct quote may be appropriate, for example 'I told him that I would not be able to do that', if it is relevant to the situation or discussion. Healy and Mulholland (2012) reflect that reporting emotion and context of speech in case recordings can be an important role for a student social worker: accurate and impartial representation of a service user's response can significantly impact on future decision making.

Accurate and objective conclusion

It is important that the case recording ends with a clear, accurate and objective conclusion, so that subsequent readers can easily see the outcomes. In Chapter Four we discussed summarising discussions, and this is very much the same philosophy: by summarising the intervention we gain clarity for ourselves and the reader. Constable (2013) recommends that the case recording provides a clear recommendation when appropriate.

ACTIVITY 9.2

CASE RECORDING 1

3 October

It was a sunny day and I took my time approaching the blue-doored house. I knocked on the door and rang the bell. J opened the door with a bright rejoinder and we reflected on the turn of the weather. I noticed a little girl walk past and wave at J, a right bobbly dazzler she was. On entering the drawing room, I noticed the atrocious stench of dog poo. Can the woman not smell it? Poor darling.

I turned the conversation to the issue in hand: that of her son's handicap and how she is making it worse. I explained all about the Social Model of Disability and how she needs to enable him not disable him. Whilst she looked a bit befuddled, I assured her that I could get some reading for her on the matter.

I asked about H's health- all fine, some appointments coming up; his education- he's still not attending; and the temper tantrums- still happening despite my advice last week.

J is still fighting with her neighbour. I told her again not to. I did wonder if perhaps she could just tidy the garden a bit to try to resolve the issue? I'd struggle with her as a neighbour. Overall J was clearly incapable of parenting H effectively.

H was upstairs, but it's too much for him to come downstairs, so I'll catch him another time.

I told J about the ICPC and the need for her to attend. I wasn't convinced of her interest in the meeting, we shall see.

- Think about the concerns that this recording raises.
- Can you re-write it more appropriately?

CASE RECORDING 2

3 October 2016

Present: Jackie, Harry, Jill Fi (student social worker)

I called to Jackie's huse to discuss the Initail Child Pretection Conferance next week. I went through the repirt with Jackei, explain some of the isssues that she riased.

I raitarated our concurns about the need to supppirt Harry's disibility to meet his neds, and that we wud supirt her to do that. I explained that the Child Pretection Plan wud set out how we wud help her and the expoctions that we would have of her.

I asked Jakie about her neighbours. She felt that things were still antagnistic, and we talked about if she cud think of anything to do, including tiedying the garden.

I saw Hairy alone upstairs. He sed that he is happy, although he misses attending skool. He sed he wanted to see his friends soon. I told him about a social grup, which she seemd keen on and asked me to find out about.

Actions: arrange transport for Jacie to confarance on Tuesday

: Get information about social group to Hairy

- Think about the issues that this recording raises
- Can you re-write it more appropriately?
- Which one are you happier with?

Both recordings have their faults, but if you reflect on the issues discussed above when you record, you should be able to write to a higher standard than this.

OTHER FACTORS TO CONSIDER

Opinion?

There are two simple perspectives on including your professional opinion in case recording: you should never do so or you can with care. You should refer to your agency's policy and philosophy on this for clarity. However, in most social work agencies, there is a clear philosophy that stating your professional judgement, based on your knowledge and experience, is acceptable, provisional to it being clearly labelled as opinion, and that it is both non-judgemental and backed by the reasons for that perspective. However, you must never include your personal opinion.

Evidence-based practice

In the early years of this century, the philosophy of evidence-based practice, that is, utilising theory and research to support your judgement, became popular. It has had some backlash and is probably best reserved for report and assessment writing, as discussed in the next chapter.

Recording ethical dilemmas and sensitive issues

There are times as a student social worker when you will be unsure. You may have to deal with an ethical dilemma. On the one hand, you might feel that Jack should live with his mother, but on the other you can see the benefits of Jack living with his father. It is acceptable to outline your dilemma in a case recording, but ensure that you represent both perspectives clearly, concisely and objectively, utilising facts and stating when it is opinion so that the future reader can see your thinking.

When recording sensitive issues, write the case record and re-read it to ensure that it is confidential where it should be, aware of and respects the service user, and cannot be mis-interpreted (see later in this chapter). Sometimes asking a neutral person to read it can give you some objectivity, but because of confidentiality concerns, ensure that they are a colleague. O'Rourke (2010) identified a reluctance in some student social workers to address sensitive issues, and identified a coping strategy of putting them, albeit tactfully, in case notes rather than assessments, as case notes were viewed to be less accessible by service users. However, a good ethical rule to work by is that if you feel uncomfortable about a service user seeing the recording, then you should consider why this is so. Chapter Six examines the necessity of an open and honest relationship, however hard that might be, and the skills that you need to develop to enable this to happen.

Information on family members

If you work with a group of siblings, it can be tempting to cut and paste comments about one sibling to the next. However, it is very important that only the information relevant to that person is included on their file. Information about another family member would only be included if it were relevant to the service user about whom you were writing. For example, on a looked-after child visit to a group of siblings in a foster placement, there may be a number of common themes, but each individual child's health, education needs, etc. should be recorded in their own file only. This can also apply to adults in group living situations, or where both partners in a couple have a social worker.

ACTIVITY 9.3

When you next attend a tutorial, write up your experience for a colleague. Think about the important issues that need to be recorded as clearly and concisely as you feel able.

When your colleague reads your recording of the tutorial, do they agree that it is an accurate representation of the tutorial? Do they remember things differently? Would they have added or left out anything?

The final point about a case recording is that it is hard to be objective. Social workers will notice different things, interpret things differently, and have different styles. You will not only need to read your agency's recordings to get an idea of how they should be written but also develop your own style of recording.

WRITTEN COMMUNICATION WITH SERVICE USERS AND PROFESSIONALS

Whilst the importance of face-to-face communication is reflected on throughout this book, there is also much communication with service users and other professionals that is of a written nature. Telephone discussion is still an important aspect of the student social worker's repertoire, but there are many times when a written communication is both appropriate and efficient. With the range of modern technology, a person-centred approach must be considered: what does the service user prefer? There is no point insisting on using WhatsApp with an older service user who does not have the internet, or writing a letter to a homeless service user. However, you also have to be aware of both your agency's policy and resources to ensure that you are communicating within agreed standards. Healy and Mulholland (2012) remind us that we represent both ourselves and our agency when we produce written communication.

Letters

Whilst now referred to as *snail mail* in some areas, a formal letter can communicate an important message effectively. In social work the letter is often used as an introductory tool, as discussed in Chapter One, and also as a medium for delivering a formal message to a service user, for example about a meeting or decision outcome.

In a letter, it is important to ensure that you are aware of the agency protocol. Is there a headed paper, a font, or a style that is expected to be utilised on any letters representing the agency? A letter often utilises more formal language: avoid the use of text speak within a letter. Healy and Mulholland (2012) argue that letters should follow a formulaic process, with the formal address of sendee and recipient, reason for communication, body of communication and summary, with a formal ending utilising established letter-writing etiquette.

Text

In today's society, communication by text has become the norm. You only have to sit on the bus or in a café to see that everyone is talking to each other by text, often when they are close by to each other. As such, it has become normal to text service users to arrange a visit or to confirm some information. However, there are a couple of things to consider when texting service users. Firstly, you still need to keep professional boundaries: ensure that you use an office mobile and not your own, in office hours (you are not accessible at weekends to receive an update), and ensure that you utilise full words not text speak. For example, 'Can I com 2 c u 2moro? 3? Thx P' appears informal. How will you end a text communication? It is appropriate to provide your name, but often service users will have your contact details saved. A small recent survey by Klin et al. (2015) identified that ending a text with a full stop seemed insincere, but ending it with an exclamation mark made the sender sound sincere. Klin et al. (2015) argued that punctuation has come to replace emotion and meaning in the brief and abbreviated text speak.

The other point you will need to consider is whether you will record your text communications. You should treat them like a telephone call and record them within the case recording. And remember that the positive aspect of text communication, accessibility for the service user, can also be your enemy. Ensure that you do not text one service user whilst visiting another, or text the wrong service user.

Social media

There is a clear and growing societal trend for communication utilising social media: WhatsApp, Instagram, Snapchat, to name a few. So long as the service user has an internet connection, this communication is free and immediate, which has obvious attractions. The issues remain as discussed in the section above on texting. Remember your privacy settings if using social media communication, and have a professional account that is not used personally. (Also remember that you cannot make an oppressive or inappropriate comment on social media in private any more than you would whilst visiting a service user.) Social media will also need to be used within your organisational structures and procedures. You will need to be aware of the ethics of social media communication, in that it is open and universal: chats can be joined by a service user's friends, information can be freely shared and control is minimal. One could argue that this is a good thing: the service user has greater control and choice, but the student social worker has to be aware of the ethics of confidentiality and rights. Does a mother and carer of an adult with a disability have the right to share service information that you have shared on social media?

Email

As a student social worker, you will utilise email throughout your day. Social work offices come with a computer and email address as standard, and much communication is undertaken by email, particularly information sharing between professionals, colleagues and managers.

There are several factors to consider in email communication. Many of the rules for recording still apply: the communication still needs to be clear, concise, grammatically correct and spelled appropriately, and acronyms and jargon should be avoided. Also you need to ensure that you have an electronic signature that includes your name, role and contact details, and an out-of-office automatic reply for any absences. Healy and Mulholland (2012) reflect that electronic written communication has become less formal since its initial introduction, more akin to a memo. However, good email communication should include an informal friendliness whilst retaining structure to retain professionalism. Healy and Mulholland (2102) also reflect that attachments should be utilised to share information, and that a further advantage is that emails can be sent to multiple people.

The student social worker has to be aware of the phatic conversation that also accompanies inter-professional and colleague communication. It is common for a health visitor who knew you were away last week to ask how your holiday went. However, when this email then goes on to share concerns about a service user's parenting, it will need to be added to the case file. It is clear that this is not sensitive to the service user, nor appropriate to be included, yet to amend the email is unethical.

Finally, many business sources recommend that if you cannot provide an immediate response, let the sender know that you are acknowledging their request and will get back to them shortly. We have heard of the '90 second rule': if you don't respond to an email in the first 90 seconds, it is likely you will not do so, as it will disappear into a long list of responses needed. It is therefore worth developing a habit of responding to all emails that you can do immediately, to reduce delay, avoidance and a spiraling to-do list.

REFLECTIVE TASK 9.3

- What is your preferred method of communication?
  - Do you like speaking to the person, and will always try to ring a service user or professional?
  - Do you prefer the quicker, less personal email?
  - Or do you prefer the more modern text/social media conversation?
- Does this preference effect the efficiency of your communication?

Your agency may have a policy that outlines how quickly responses must be made not only to emails but also to letters, telephone messages, etc. If you know that you favour one correspondence method more than another, let people know, but you should still check all communication methods that your agency utilises on a regular basis. And remember to check the service user's preferred communication style and utilise that. There is a notion that text/social media/email can facilitate an instance response, which can be a positive within some circles. However, ensure that you are not so tied down by immediate responses that you fail to physically interact with service users, colleague and professionals.

Confidentiality

Written communication raises a number of issues in regard to confidentiality. The first and most simple one is easy to illustrate.

REFLECTIVE TASK 9.4

You ring a service user's mobile and a stranger answers the phone. Do you leave a message that you are the service user's student social worker?

You will likely reflect that you do not know who the person is, and that without the service user's permission it would break confidentiality, or even put the service user at risk if the speaker was an alleged perpetrator of domestic abuse and the service user's partner.

REFLECTIVE TASK 9.4 CONTINUED

You text the service user. Her partner reads the text ... Have you broken confidentiality?

If the service user has given permission or prefers that you communicate by text (or social media or email or letter) then ethically this is acceptable. However, you and the service user will need to reflect on whether there are times or subjects that should not be communicated electronically, as you cannot predict who will open a text. That is not to say that you should speak in code, but that on occasions electronic communication is not appropriate.

Furthermore, as a student social worker you need to think about the confidentiality and security of your electronic gadget. Elhai and Hall (2015) argued that many of the small sample of American mental health clinicians whom they interviewed did not have password-protected mobile phones, nor did they know whether their provider was secure. Is there any difference between losing a paper file and a tablet with service user information on it? You will need to check with your agency whether you are allowed to utilise your home laptop to check emails before you do so.

And finally, Healy and Mulholland (2012) also warn of the danger that electronic communications can be forwarded to other professionals/service users/non-service users without your permission. Once an email or text has been sent you have no control of the recipient's use of it. Whilst this is also true of letters, and even repeated verbal conversation, it is useful to remember this. The important point regarding confidentiality is that you need to consider the issues, and discuss them with your agency and your service user to establish rules for safe usage.

Communication skills in written communication: utilising your listening, clarification, empathy, and challenging skills

When discussing verbal communication, we focus on the four key skills of listening, clarification, empathy and challenging, which enable us to communicate effectively. How do we utilise these skills in written communication? Firstly, we will need to listen carefully to hear what is said: ensure that our interpretation of a service user, professional or colleague's written communication conveys what was intended to be expressed. That might mean that we have to clarify throughout written conversations to ensure that we have attributed the same meaning as the writer. Secondly, we will need to have empathy for the writer, in that we will need to understand where they are coming from: that might be about understanding a medical perspective, or whether they struggle to communicate utilising written communication because of (a lack of) ability or resources. And finally, we should consider whether it is correct to challenge using a written medium. One would argue that in order to implement the issues discussed in Chapter Six that this should be done face to face with the service user or professional. However, if as a student social worker you have to challenge utilising written communication, you will need to think very carefully about the language and tone that you use to achieve this effectively and tactfully.

 COMMUNICATION SKILLS AUDIT: WRITTEN COMMUNICATION SKILLS

Finally, reflect on your strengths and areas for development in relation to written communication and identify two or three action points for you to develop (Table 9.1).

Table 9.1   Communication skills audit: written communication skills

	Strengths in written communication	Areas for development	Action points to improve written communication
Domain 1 Professionalism			
Domain 7 Intervention and skills			
Domain 8 Contexts and organisations			

CONCLUSION

Written communication with service users or professionals, or with future case social workers in case recordings, is important as it represents you and the agency for whom you work. The lack of non-verbal communication means that written communication can be misinterpreted, so care and thought must be given to clear and concise writing to ensure that an objective translation is achieved. There are many different forms of written communication, and each has its own requirements and etiquette, which are important to remember.

FURTHER READING

Frith, L. and Martin, R. (2015) *Professional Writing Skills for Student Social Workers.* Maidenhead: Open University Press.
Healy, K. and Mulholland, J. (2012) *Writing Skills for Student Social Workers.* London: Sage.

Both books provide useful advice and direction to enhance your writing skills in a breadth of areas.

CHAPTER
TEN

ASSESSMENT AND REPORT WRITING: CRITICAL ANALYSIS

Links to Knowledge and Skills Statements

Adults: role of social workers working with adults; person-centred practice; effective assessments and outcome-based support planning; direct work with individuals and families; supervision, critical reflection and analysis; organisational context; professional ethics and leadership

Children's: relationships and effective direct work; communication; child and family assessment; analysis, decision making, planning and review; role of supervision; organisational context

INTRODUCTION

The chapter will discuss assessment styles, asking the reader to reflect on their preferred style within Smale et al.'s (1993) models of assessment, and how to follow Sutton's (1994) ASPIRE (assessment, planning, intervention, review and evaluation) model of assessment. It will critically analyse evidence-based assessment writing to support an analytical perspective. It will reflect on person-centred assessment writing to ensure that service users are aware of and understand content. It will conclude by looking at reports and chronologies. However, it is important to remember that all the issues considered throughout this book are relevant to written communication: you will need to ensure that you provide transparent, unambiguous written communication that non-judgementally hears and represents the service user's perspectives for prospective readers and decision makers.

REPORTS AND ASSESSMENTS

It is helpful to reflect on the difference between a report and an assessment. An assessment is a written document that enables you to gather all information together and critically analyse the information to come to a conclusion that will recommend steps to be taken, usually in a support or care plan. This contrasts with a report, which can be seen to be a review or summary of events, often written to facilitate decision making by another party. The recommendations from an assessment may be part of a report.

Reports and assessments play an important role in social work: they summarise the work you, and others, have undertaken with the service user, represent the service user's experiences, wishes and feelings, and inform decision-making processes. This means that they have to be written in a form that is clear, concise, professional and yet accessible for both management and service users. Many of the issues discussed in the previous chapter will be relevant here, for example citing opinion versus facts.

Reports and assessments come in a variety of formats, depending on the agency and service user group with whom you work. However, they will usually have a prescribed purpose and you will be expected to utilise a prescribed format. The first port of call should be identification of an agency proforma to complete, so that you know what is expected within the document. But you should also ask if the team has an exemplar, to support your understanding of the level of detail required within each section.

ASPIRE MODEL OF ASSESSMENT

The assessment formula, that is, the process to follow to ascertain a clear assessment, has been described by Sutton (1994) as ASPIRE, and can be tracked back to its nursing origins in APIE (Yura and Walsh, 1967). It asks the assessor to work through the stages of assessment, planning, intervention, review and evaluation. Figure 10.1 on page 137 demonstrates the cyclical nature of the ASPIRE model.

Assessment: This is when you are gathering information from the service users, carers and professionals involved, using all your communication skills such as initial engagement, listening, empathy, clarifying and challenging, as well as consulting historical records within case records. Later in this chapter, the section on cognitive bias reflects on ensuring that you undertake a non-prejudicial assessment. You will be required to critically analyse all information, which may contradict each other on occasions, to form an objective conclusion and make recommendations. The assessment will inform your planning, which is the next stage.

Planning: A plan will indicate who needs to do what by when. The section on evidence-based assessments reflects on the importance of using service users' perspectives when formulating a plan. It is important to remember that goals in the plan should not just be the service user's responsibility, but that all professionals will need to be allocated tasks to empower the service user to achieve the agreed plan. Goals should be SMART (small, achievable, realistic, time-specific) targets (Doran, 1981), so that they are not overwhelming to the service user. The plan sets out your intervention.

Intervention: This is the period when you are supporting the service user to address the changes identified in the assessment and outlined in the plan. There will be a wide range of interventions, utilising several social work models and methods of intervention and all your verbal communication skills. It is important to remember to tailor the interventions to the service user's needs to gain optimum outcome. The intervention will then require to be reviewed.

Review: At regular points, the plan should be reviewed to determine if goals have been met or need adjusting from a person-centred and service-centred perspective. This will ensure that the plan remains relevant, and offers the service user regular feedback and encouragement towards their goals. The review will also provide space for evaluation. As with the assessment stage of the ASPIRE model, you will need to use all your communication skills to ensure that you hear the progress made, service user's perspective and other professionals' input.

Evaluation: This will enable you to reflect on self-evaluation and feedback from the service user (and potentially other professionals) to develop your skills further, which will enhance your ability to provide effective ongoing assessments, plans and interventions for service users.

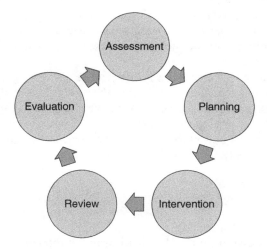

Figure 10.1 The ASPIRE model.

Figure 10.1 shows that assessment, utilising the ASPIRE model, should be a fluid event. *Working Together* recognises the importance of seeing assessment as:

> a dynamic process, which analyses and responds to the changing nature and level of need and/or risk faced by the child. (Department for Education, 2015: 20)

The very task of assessment inevitably changes the service user's life as they talk about themselves and reflect upon their strengths and areas for development. Further to this the implementation of the plan impacts on them as they address concerns and make decisions. These, one hopes, positive changes will inevitably necessitate further assessment of need and the plan adapted accordingly, which will enable the intervention to be adjusted to meet the new areas of development. Even if the planned intervention has no visible impact on the service user, in itself informs the assessment and will shape future service delivery. As such, an assessment can only ever be seen as a snapshot of a service user's life. It is rare that a service user's circumstances remain the same. For example, Case study 10.1 shows that, as Harold's life changes, so do the student social worker's responses. She continually reviews, reassesses and updates his plan.

CASE STUDY 10.1

Harold's health has deteriorated due to persistent alcohol misuse and impacted on his ability to meet his own needs. He requests that his needs should be assessed to determine which support services would be of benefit to him. The student social worker meets with him to discuss his needs, and identifies that his son is a key carer. The student social worker also meets with the son, to establish his ability to provide care, and if he requires support. The student social worker establishes from the community nurse that Harold's physical health is deteriorating, and gathers information about his alcohol misuse from the substance misuse worker.

The student social worker writes a needs assessment and recommends a care and support plan to supplement the son's care of Harold to enable him to remain in his family home.

Harold's physical health deteriorates further, and he displays signs of dementia. His son reports that on one occasion Harold has left the family home at night and has been found several streets away asking people for money for a drink. Again, the student social worker visits Harold to gather information on his wishes and feelings, and talks to all the professionals involved to determine their perspective. The assessment and care plan are subsequently updated.

BIAS

Similarly to the discussion about clarification in Chapter Four, it is important to undertake an assessment from a non-prejudiced perspective, yet the student social worker is also asked to begin an assessment with a hypothesis. You would be encouraged to formulate that hypothesis from a strengths-based perspective: that Harold would be able to live independently with the right support, for example. You will be expected, as part of the initial information-gathering stage of the assessment, to read historical and/or recent case notes, and to discuss the service user with other professionals involved to ensure that you have a holistic overview, which will begin to confirm or alter your hypothesis. Mainstone (2014) argues that, by gathering and analysing different perspectives from different professionals, the student social worker will have a greater understanding of all the issues that impact on the service user. It will enable the assessor to identify risks and strengths within the family. It is like a jigsaw puzzle: only when all the pieces are put together can the risks and resilience factors be seen. You will draw on all the skills outlined in Chapter Nine when you are gathering information from other professionals.

However, it is hard not to make judgements, and often negative ones, as student social workers only receive referrals when there are concerns from the professionals involved. As a skilled assessing social worker you will be reading and hearing information that influences you to think in a particular direction. An emotionally intelligent, assessing student social worker will need to maintain an open mind, whilst weighing *all* the information you receive, to adjust your hypothesis to come to an informed, critical conclusion.

CASE STUDY 10.2

Helena was placed for adoption, but sadly the placement was not successful. Although her parents had been assessed previously as unable to affect changes to their parenting in the required timescale within the care proceedings, this placement breakdown enabled the father to apply to be reassessed as some time had elapsed.

On reading the files it was clear that Helena's father had misused and prioritised drugs, and had not been able to parent Helena safely. The student social worker was asked 'as a formality' to assess Helena's father, with no optimism that he would be a suitable carer for this child, who had been emotionally damaged by the placement breakdown. However, when the assessing student social worker attended the father's home, it was clear that he had addressed his drug misuse issues and was in a stable relationship. This altered her hypothesis, and the assessment proceeded to assess his (and his partner's) ability to meet Helena's needs. As a result of this assessment, Helena was successfully placed with her father and his partner.

It is important that, despite having an original working hypothesis, the assessing student social worker was able to respond to the new information without bias to ensure an outcome that prioritised safe family placement. Clapson (2016) reflects that it is natural to see more of what you are looking for (confirmation bias).

He also argues that we are instinctively committed to the first piece of information we receive, and have to be persuaded away from it. Had the student social worker arrived and the father not been at home, she might have taken this as a sign that he was disorganised because of ongoing drug use and confirmed her hypothesis. Clapson argues that to avoid confirmation bias preventing a fair assessment, the student social worker needs to take time to reflect and to ask themselves challenging questions that counter their own hypothesis.

You will also need to reflect on your personal biases: can you really assess fairly a father who is on the Sex Offenders list? You will need to focus on yourself and, with every intervention with a service user, ensure that the assessment is not biased because of personal feelings or values. That is not to say that you will or should never have a bias, but to say that you need to be aware of the natural biases that everyone has.

As discussed in Chapter One, the important point in both these areas is that of your emotional intelligence: your recognising and being aware of your bias. By being aware of potential bias, you will be able to undertake an open, objective assessment.

EVIDENCE-BASED ASSESSMENTS

Although the argument for evidence-based practice gained strength in the 1990s, it was the introduction of the assessment framework guidance (Department of Health, 2000) that endorsed its regular use in assessments. Evidence-based practice is when the student social worker draws on existing research and social work knowledge to inform their practice. National bodies such as the National Institute for Health and Care Excellence (NICE), Research in Practice (RIP), and the Social Care Institute for Excellence (SCIE) have been set up to support easy access to social work research and developments for student social workers. Fisher (2016) reflects on the changes over recent years in the definition of what counts as evidence-based: from dependence on published social work research to also incorporating service user perspectives and student social workers' experience.

A good social work assessment should see the service user as the expert in themselves and the student social worker as the expert in their field. The student social worker will be required to gather the information that the service user has about their own life, and their wishes and feelings so that the plan can be owned by the service user. There is much research, particularly the Transtheoretical Stages of Change model (often known as the Cycle of Change) (Prochaska and DiClemente, 1983), that shows us that until a service user is ready to change we cannot enforce change on them, so that a plan that reflects the service user's current position is critical to a successful intervention.

The assessing student social worker, then, must be an expert in critically analysing the service user's history to recognise the impact on their life, as well as reflecting on their wishes and feelings, and drawing on their own knowledge and expertise, to formulate the most appropriate plan for a successful intervention.

REFLECTIVE TASK 10.1

You go to the doctor and he prescribes a medicine for your health complaint. Do you prefer that he should:

- Be able to tell you that there is research showing this medicine works for this complaint, and that whilst there are known side effects, they are within agreed guidelines

or

- Tell you that this is a new, untested drug, which, he has heard anecdotally, might work for a similar complaint?

Most of you will prefer to know that the help you receive is based on research and knowledge. Social work interventions should be seen the same way: you should be able to clarify and justify why you have chosen a particular intervention with research and theory. This will highlight for you the importance of understanding how theory underpins your practice, and, for the future, of keeping abreast of current social work theory and research. You may be thinking at this point, how do you ensure that your assessments are evidence-based? You will need to ensure that within any critical analysis sections of your assessment, if you assert an opinion, you should validate this with theoretical reasoning.

CASE STUDY 10.2 CONTINUED

I recommend that Helena's father and his partner are suitable carers for Helena because it is evident that the father no longer misuses, or indeed uses, drugs. If referenced to the Transtheoretical Stages of Change model (Prochaska and DiClemente, 1983), it can be seen that the father has been in maintenance for a substantial period of time and has clear coping strategies for if he lapsed or were tempted to lapse.

In this case study, the student social worker informs the court of her recommendation, utilising an evidence-based approach. She can explain her reasoning for her decision, which strengthen her recommendation.

But be careful: do not 'try to be clever'. If you cite theory, you must understand it, use it correctly, and be prepared to be able to verbalise your reasoning behind your utilisation of it. Plafky (2016) reminds us that knowledge must be used critically, that is, that we should think about why we are using a theory or piece of research to support our decision, and that we need to consider knowledge from both social work and other disciplines to ensure a holistic response.

QUESTIONING, PROCEDURAL AND EXCHANGE MODELS OF ASSESSMENT

Smale et al. (1993) developed three different approaches the student social worker could take when completing an assessment with a service user:

- The questioning model: where the assessor is seen as the expert and the lead and follows their agenda to gather information, often asking set questions.
- The procedural model: where the assessor utilises the questioning model to determine if their agency's criteria are met for service provision.
- The exchange model: where the service user is seen as the expert, and the assessor's role is to support the service user to find solutions and maximise potential outcomes.

Clearly, the exchange model method is a person-centred approach to assessment, and fits well with the discussion in the other chapters in this book. Whilst this book cannot focus on different intervention methods, the style of solution-focused (de Shazer, 1985) and task-centred (Doel and Marsh, 1992) interventions can be seen to utilise the exchange model of assessment, as they see the service user as an expert in themselves, and the student social worker supports them to identify their strengths to develop their resilience to problems.

Nevertheless, as a student social worker, you will experience the ethical dilemma that we have also discussed earlier in the book, for example the dilemma around whom you are recording for (see Chapter Nine), that sometimes your professional values regarding working in a person-centred way may conflict with your professional expectations to conform to the agency's protocol. Some assessments require a simple procedural model assessment designed to establish whether or not the service user is eligible for services. This requires the student social worker to work through set questions to establish facts. However, even within a procedural model of assessment, the service user's wishes and feelings should be sought and recorded.

CASE STUDY 10.1 CONTINUED

Imagine you are the student social worker in this case study, undertaking Harold's initial needs assessment. Make a list of the people whom you feel you should talk to and what information would you want from each person.

- Would your approach be different from anyone else's?
- Is your agenda different with different people?

Naturally, your response will be different to a service user and colleague or involved professional. When talking to Harold you will ensure that you speak in a jargon-free manner, which you may not need to do when talking to a professional. Nevertheless, we would strongly urge you to ensure that if you are prepared to voice an opinion to a professional, ensure that you are also prepared to voice it to the service user to ensure an open and honest working relationship.

UNDERTAKING AN ASSESSMENT IN A PERSON-CENTRED MANNER

Mainstone (2014) argues that by collating the information from all perspectives a holistic assessment can be undertaken. She argues that when working with a family it is critical to ensure that the child or young person is spoken to and heard, as they will experience the situation from their own individual perspective. For example, issues of resilience will impact on their experience of a situation and will be critical to informing a plan as a result of the assessment. The issues remain valid when reflecting on the needs of a service user whose carer is also their advocate: the service user's views also need to be heard to establish authenticity and lack of bias. An assessment should contain different perspectives than your own, as it should represent the perspectives of the service user and any other relevant family members and professionals. When expressing opinion always ensure that you are clear it is opinion and not fact, and its source.

You will draw on all the skills outlined in Chapters Two to Seven when you are gathering information with service users, carers, relatives and children. There are a few simple techniques that you can undertake to make sure that every service user is respected within an assessment, irrespective of the model of assessment you undertake, which follow the communication techniques that the first half of the book has followed.

Initial engagement: Firstly, you should always ensure that the person understands the process and possible outcomes. Remember, the service user may not have the same agenda as you, as discussed in Chapter Two on initial engagements, so understanding a service user's frustration through preparatory empathy will be useful. The discussions and reflections about barriers to communication in Chapter Eight should be considered within any assessment process.

Listening: The philosophy of gathering information from everyone underpins an assessment, so the student social worker must *listen* to each and every perspective, and ensure that it is represented within the assessment document. As the next stage is to critically reflect on the information that is gathered, the accuracy of your listening will be imperative to enabling you to balance different perspectives and information from all involved.

Clarification: In order to ensure that you have listened effectively, it will be imperative to clarify your understanding of the service user's and other agencies' perspectives. The assessment document will record for posterity how the service user felt or perceived an event, and can be used in future decision-making processes.

Empathy: In order to assess effectively, the student social worker must be empathic in their communication, as it is only by being aware of the service user's feelings that we can endeavour to engage them in reflective discussion as to their life, both current and historical, to enable us to undertake a thorough holistic assessment.

Challenging: In order for an assessment to be effective, the student social worker will also have to challenge the service user's dialogue. This can be because the service user is not being open and honest within the assessment process, or because they are not being honest with themselves. We believe that a comprehensive assessment is in itself a therapeutic intervention, as the service user is asked to look back at their own life and reflect on decisions made, or look at current events and their role within them. By the student social worker challenging their assumptions and perspectives of events, the service user is asked to examine their own constructions of their reality. The assessment can reflect any shifts the service user makes within the assessment process.

HOW TO WRITE AN ASSESSMENT

As discussed above, an assessment will follow set criteria, a similar pattern, despite having different content, purpose and agenda. Initially, factual information about the service user(s), for example date of birth, address, family composition, etc., should be provided, to enable the reader to see clearly the context of the situation. This would be followed by a significant section on information gathered, which could include information from service users, carers, children, professionals, and/or case files on all relevant areas, depending on the assessment. Dyke (2016) reminds us that an assessment should not contain, what he calls, categories. He argues that utilising phrases leads to a lack of clarity, for example 'domestic abuse' can represent a host of verbal and physical aggression situations and leaves the reader unclear as to the level and frequency of domestic abuse and the impact it had on the victim. It is important that the assessment contains clear, specific description of the issues that the service user faces and the impact that it has. Of course, it is also important to provide clear and specific detail of the strengths and resilience that a service user has. However, Dyke also adds a word of caution that this section should not be overly long, or it will lose its impact.

This should be followed by a further comprehensive section that analyses the information provided in the previous section. It could be argued that the analytical section is the most important section of an assessment because it is the one that pulls the information together and, as discussed above, makes the complete picture visible. Ofsted (2015c) argued that social work assessments of children in need are improving in quality, but would be enhanced further with analysis of the gathered information to recommend a clear plan. The analysis should consider the service user's behaviours from a multi-layered perspective and should consider the following issues:

- What personal issues are impacting on the service user?
- What impact is this having on the service user and/or other members of the family?
- What triggers relapse of behaviour?
- What strengths does the service user utilise as coping strategies?
- What resources does the service user have access to?
- What is stopping the service user from accessing and utilising support services?

A good analysis will help the student social worker to understand the service user's behaviour, and therefore enable them to recommend the most appropriate way to support a service user. This can be done through individual reflection, but *Working Together* (Department for Education, 2015) recommends that supervision is used to reflect on information gathered to strengthen the analytical perspective. Also utilise peer support, which can be just as effective. Often talking through issues enables the student social worker to make sense of them, and an objective perspective can clarify or challenge your assumptions and analysis. Frith and Martin (2015) recommend making a list of factors from all perspectives will also enable you to come to a clear conclusion.

The assessment should end with recommendations or a plan. As discussed above, this should be person-centred and include achievable targets that nominate all involved (service user and professionals) to undertake tasks to empower the service user to evidence change.

Finally, good communication is the key to a good assessment. Engaging and communicating with service users and professionals to gather information should contribute to a well-written assessment that communicates the service user's needs effectively. Dyke (2016) reminds us that our assessments should be jargon-free, and should be easily readable. He argues that if service users do not find the assessment accessible it is unlikely that it will be effective as it disengages the service user.

ACTIVITY 10.1

Using the following headings, write a brief assessment of the current living arrangements of your sister (or best friend, brother, or a made-up acquaintance):

- Personal details
- Personal history
- Current living arrangements
- Analysis: strengths
- Areas for development
- Recommendations

It might be an idea not to share your recommendations with the person if it is contentious.

This task is aimed to help you reflect on your assessment skills to inform your communication skills audit at the end of the chapter. What did you write clearly and concisely? Which areas need further thought to make them effective?

REPORTS AND CHRONOLOGIES

By contrast to an assessment, a report is a compilation of facts and events, to enable a decision to be made. Effectively it is a review or summary of the information available. It enables the reader to view all the information in one document.

A chronology is a clear, concise report that provides a summary of key events. It is often written in bullet or box form. Laming (2003, recommendation 58) endorsed that every child's file needs to have a chronology clearly available to enable decision making through visible identification of patterns of behaviour. This had been advocated in previous government guidelines, such as the assessment framework guidance (Department of Health, 2000). As a newly allocated student social worker you will be expected to acquaint yourself with the facts of the case (as discussed in Chapter Two), and a clear chronology enables you to familiarise yourself with the timeline, interventions delivered, periods of improvement and periods of risk. Dyke (2016) argues that reading a chronology prepares you for an initial visit and shows that you respect and value the service user by having knowledge of their individual situation. He also argues that before any initial visit on receipt of a referral, the student social worker should undertake an informal chronology whilst accumulating and ordering information to inform their planning process of how to proceed.

Within a chronology, the student social worker will determine the relevant details to include, and provide concise, clear information.

ACTIVITY 10.2

Review the (limited) list of events from Helena's file: which events would you include in a chronology?

Initial referral	Child protection medical	Home visit
School visit	Discussion with manager	Helena born
Telephone call to mental health support worker	Mum ended relationship with partner	Office visit: mum dna
Placed for adoption	Placement broke down	Birthday party

It is difficult to know what not to include, but the important events are Helena's date of birth, the referral and medical, and the relationship ending. It is not that the other events are unimportant, instead that they are the cement that holds together the more critical moments. But in decision making, it is the critical moments we need to examine. One could debate whether mother not attending an appointment could or should go in, but it would generally be better to leave engagement patterns for a report.

Whilst a report would consider including a chronology – so that behaviour patterns could be seen – it would also include information on a variety of other relevant issues, for example, a statement of fact on engagement with the agency would be of merit if it were relevant to the decision-making process. A report would detail different areas of relevant information and summarise it for the reader in more detail than a chronology. For example, there could be sections on Helena's education, her father's abstinence from drug use, housing conditions, etc. The report could end with recommendations for the reader to consider, which could inform their decision-making process. However, a report would require the writer to retain a factual objectivity.

ASSESSMENT AND REPORT WRITING CHECKLIST

- Ensure that your writing is clear, to ensure it is not open to interpretation.
- Organise evidence to enable a clear flowing structure (this might be chronologically or thematically arranged).
- Ensure evidence is presented clearly and concisely.
- Do not pick evidence: evidence that does not support your recommendation shows that you have undertaken a fair information-gathering task, and enables clear, informed decision making.
- Ensure the voice of the service user is present in the report.
- Proofread for grammar, spellings and structure.

(Adapted from Healy and Mulholland, 2012: 91)

Remember that, be it an assessment or a report, the service user should be provided with the written document in plenty of time for them to review the paperwork before it is utilised. This will mean ensuring that you plan in time to allow for this to happen and adjustments to be made at their request. A service user will need time not only to read the document but also to reflect on it, so 10 minutes before the meeting it will be used in is insufficient time for them to read and digest it. You will also need to reflect on if the report needs printing in larger print or translating to ensure that the service user is able to access it.

COMMUNICATION SKILLS AUDIT: ASSESSMENT AND REPORT WRITING SKILLS

Finally, reflect on your strengths and areas for development in relation to assessment and report writing and identify two or three action points for you to develop (Table 10.1).

Table 10.1   Communication skills audit: assessment and report writing skills

	Strengths in assessment and report writing	Areas for development	Action points to improve assessment and report writing
Domain 5 Knowledge			
Domain 6 Critical reflection and analysis			
Domain 7 Intervention and skills			
Domain 8 Contexts and Organisations			

CONCLUSION

The assessment of a service user is critical to the success of your intervention. Without an understanding of where the service user is, the factors affecting them, and their wishes, feelings and needs, an appropriate support plan cannot be made. You will need to ensure that you have a holistic perspective: gathering the family's or carer's wishes and feelings using all the communication techniques discussed earlier in the book, and all involved professionals' information, even though they may contradict and necessitate reflection on the complex ethical dilemmas that emerge. As in the previous chapter, clear and concise assessment writing avoids confusion, and is a skill to develop. Critical analysis should be supported with evidence-based theory and research, and all conclusions should be shared with the service user in an accessible manner.

Reports should be a summary of events to facilitate decision making. They should also be written in a clear and concise manner and shared with service users appropriately.

FURTHER READING

Dyke, C. (2016) *Writing Analytical Assessments in Social Work*. Northwich: Critical Publishing.
Mainstone, F. (2014) *Mastering Whole Family Assessment in Social Work*. London: Jessica Kingsley.

Both these books consider the specific skills required by social workers to produce good-quality and productive assessments.

INTER-PROFESSIONAL
COMMUNICATION

Links to Knowledge and Skills Statements

Adults: role of social workers working with adults; effective assessments and outcome-based support planning; organisational context; professional ethics and leadership

Children's: relationships and effective direct work; communication; analysis, decision making, planning and review; organisational context

INTRODUCTION

Following a brief reflection on some of the reasons why inter-professional working can be challenging, this chapter will aim to highlight the skills you need. Clearly there is much common ground between the skills needed in inter-professional communication and the skills needed in other areas of social work practice, so after some initial context, this chapter will follow the step-wise structure of this book: initial engagement, listening, empathy, clarification and challenging. The focus will be on the interpersonal aspects of communication. As McCray (2009) states, communication within a multi-professional environment requires similar skills to those adopted when working with service users and carers.

THE INTER-PROFESSIONAL CONTEXT AND ISSUES FOR SOCIAL WORKERS

Regardless of the setting, student social workers on placement and qualified workers are expected to work closely with a range of different professionals. You will be expected to communicate in a manner that is both effective and professional. As has been commented by a number of authors, such as Bamford (1990), no single profession can provide all the necessary skills and resources to assist service users: it generally takes a combination and effective communication is central. *Working Together* to *Safeguard Children* (2015) reiterates this, stating that:

> Ultimately, effective safeguarding of children can only be achieved by putting children at the centre of the system, and by every individual and agency playing their full part, working together to meet the needs of our most vulnerable children.

> (Department for Education, 2015: 8)

Each professional adds information to the holistic assessment like a jigsaw piece, to ensure that the whole picture can be seen. It also is clear that it is only by professionals working together, utilising their specialist skills, knowledge and resources, that a child or adult service user can be supported and safeguarded.

The professions that you will be interacting with will depend on your service user group and the needs and requirements of individuals. Social workers may work within a team with the same inter-professional colleagues, more typical of adult services, or they may work with members of other professions on a case-by-case basis, interacting at key points, more typical of children's services. There are constant changes in the nature of inter-professional working due to evolving government policy and legislation, in terms of what is deemed to be good practice, combined with more local considerations about what is the most preferred or cost-effective way of working. Independent of the particular model in operation, social work has previously been described as the 'glue' that binds other professions together (Craig and Muskat, 2013).

Students can rapidly become overwhelmed by some of the complexities involved in inter-professional working, for example communication issues, the organisation of services and the context of practice. It is only when working directly with service users that some of the realities become apparent and it is important not to underestimate the complexity of the issue. The value of working with other professionals has long been recognised; it was advocated in the Younghusband Report (1959, cited in Crawford, 2012: 4), but a recent National Audit Office report (2017) highlights that there are still many difficulties related to the integration of health and social services. It pays to remember that the overall aim of inter-professional work-ing is to bring services and professionals together to improve outcomes for service users requiring social and/or health care services.

REFLECTIVE TASK 11.1

Think about a discussion you were part of where people had different perspectives, opinions, ideas or values. This can be in any context.

- How did you feel about expressing yourself?
- Were you able to confidently 'hold your own' or did you hold back, preferring to let others do the talking?

As a social worker, you will be expected to represent your employing agency and, on occasions, advocate for your service user with other agencies. You will need to ensure your voice is heard, whilst listening to others' perspectives, and sometimes this will be challenging and difficult.

Given the predominance of the approach and the fact that it is far from new, it might be imagined that the skills and knowledge required should pose little diffi-culty, certainly for qualified practitioners, if not for students in training. Why then, it could be asked, are there so many difficulties in practice? When things go seriously wrong on an individual case level, in relation to an adult or a child, reasons such as difficulties in communication, inter-agency co-operation and collaboration are com-monly cited in investigative reports (see Adebowale, 2013 and various LSCB reports such as Oxfordshire LSCB, 2014 and Isle of Wight LSCB, 2014).

Cameron et al. (2013) highlight a number of factors identified in a range of other studies in relation to what helps and what hinders joint and integrated working between health and social care services. For example, Christiansen and Roberts (2005), Peck et al. (2001) and Kharicha et al. (2005) have all examined value differences between professional groups and the impact this has on inte-grated working. In particular, Scragg (2006) noted that one aspect of social work values – adherence to the social model – can cause issues in health teams that favour the medical model. (For a discussion of the social model, please refer to Oliver, 2013.) Scragg suggested that this can lead to the social work contribution being given less value or weight. There is a fuller exploration of the issue of barri-ers to communication in Chapter Eight, and much of this discussion also applies to inter-professional communication.

As a student social worker, you will have developed your communication skills, as you progressed through this book and other means. It is now time to think about how they apply to inter-professional communication. It may be worth linking back to the relevant chapter to remind you of the key issues for each skill discussed below.

INITIAL ENGAGEMENT

The saying 'You never get a second chance to make a first impression' quoted in Chapter Two may be a truism but many believe it. Arguably, it applies to work with service users as well as other professionals. The first contact with other professionals may be in person, on the telephone, or increasingly by email. It may be the start of a brief period of contact, a one-off or a much longer piece of contact, and the length of the period of contact may be unknown at the start of the piece of work. Taking this further, imagine you are a social work student on placement, joining an established inner-city inter-professional mental health team whose members are as described in Case study 11.1.

CASE STUDY 11.1

A PLACEMENT IN A COMMUNITY MENTAL HEALTH TEAM (CMHT)

The team you join consists of the following members of staff. Margaret is an experienced community mental health nurse who previously worked on an acute mental health admission ward, becoming a ward sister. In addition to her nursing degree, she is trained in cognitive behavioural therapy and holds a caseload of 40, mainly service users with long-term mental health needs and complex medication regimens. She generally has at least one student nurse whom she mentors and who accompanies her during the working day.

Dr Ahmed is the team's consultant psychiatrist, who trained first in general medicine and surgery and has a further four years of specialist psychiatric training. He treats both in- and out-patients, many of whom have problems related to their income or housing situation. He is assisted by a junior doctor, who is mainly ward-based, and an associate specialist, also medically qualified, who has completed a number of years of academic and clinical training in psychiatry. There may additionally be a medical student on a short rotation.

Mike is an approved mental health professional and mental health social worker, who carries out many assessments under the Mental Health Act 1983 (as amended in 2007). He also carries out other statutory functions such as report writing for mental health review tribunals and has a caseload of long-term users of mental health services. He has a social work degree and has completed approved mental health professional training as a postgraduate qualification.

In reality, a CMHT would have more members and would be drawn from an even wider range of professional groupings; it is also likely that there would be more than one representative of many of the professions. A CMHT is an example of an inter-professional team that is usually based at the same office base and may increasingly also share a management or supervisory structure. White and Featherstone (2005) note that co-location in itself does not, however, necessarily lead to better working relationships.

REFLECTIVE TASK 11.2

- What feelings might you have about joining such a team as described in case study 11.1? Why might this be important?
- How might this affect your first contacts with the team?
- How might you manage any expectations or anxieties you may have?
- What do you think each of the other team members would be expecting from you? Why?

You may not have much experience or knowledge of how such teams operate, but that is fine. This can often be the case when starting a new job.

In contrast to the largely observational placements of nursing and medical students, from an early stage in their practice placement, particularly if it is a final placement, social work students are expected to carry out assessments and interventions independently, albeit under supervision, which may not be direct. This means that other professionals may be surprised, or even reluctant, to see you taking the social work lead, as they have different expectations. Furthermore, the predominant theoretical models of social work could broadly be described as social in orientation, for example Oliver et al. (2012) in relation to health and disability, the recovery approach (Deegan, 1988) and Anthony (1993) in relation to mental health and restorative practice in relation to children's work. (For a thorough overview, see Hopkins, 2016.) By contrast, professionals from other disciplines may emphasise other ways of understanding human behaviour and experiences, such as psychological theories or understanding derived from biology or genetics.

REFLECTIVE TASK 11.3

- Does this information change the way you begin to engage with the team where you are to do your placement? How?
- Do you feel more or less confident?
- Consider how you might begin to explain your perspective and future role within the team.

There now follows some further information about some of the issues common in inter-professional working.

CASE STUDY 11.1 CONTINUED

Andy, a 25-year-old White British male, is referred for social work involvement following an out-patient appointment. He lives at home with his retired parents. He spends most of the time in his bedroom, playing online computer games. He showers perhaps once a month, and his room is littered with dirty clothes and the cartons of take-away food that he has had delivered. He was diagnosed with schizophrenia when he was 18 years old and has had several hospital admissions. He has never had a job. Andy has frequent arguments with his parents over his lifestyle choices and they feel that they want him to live somewhere else. Your practice educator, Mike, decides that you should be allocated Andy's case.

Putting aside for one moment issues related to how you would assess the situation, one of your first tasks will be to negotiate the dynamics of the inter-professional team. Dr Ahmed suggests it might be appropriate for you to find a hostel placement for Andy but is a little worried that because your social work placement is only for four months, you may not be able to see the whole process through. Margaret, the community mental health nurse, has a similar view and is also surprised that you have been asked to take the case on yourself without direct supervision. In her view, Andy's needs are rather complex, as is his family situation. She is also particularly concerned about his compliance with his medication regimen if he leaves home.

REFLECTIVE TASK 11.4

- What are your initial thoughts about taking on Andy's case?
- What considerations are there in relation to communication with other members of the inter-professional team?
- What communication methods are most suitable?
- How would you handle these initial differences of opinion?

There are probably going to be further differences as your work progresses and you are also likely to have to bear in mind the working practices, views and opinions of other agencies such as housing providers. Through your reflective work, it is likely that you will identify a number of differences between the training, focus, orientation and value bases of the different professions involved. These are quite extensive, but on a positive note they greatly enrich the service provided to the 'patients' or service users who are in receipt of that service. Therefore:

- Remember that a major part of your role is to find out what Andy wants, and to represent his needs and requirements. You also have to take account of his parents' situation. Fundamentally, you need to remain rooted in the social model, keeping the views of the service user at the heart of any assessment and intervention. You need to listen to and acknowledge your colleagues' opinions, but ultimately you may form a different opinion and recommend an alternative course of action.

- First impressions are important. It would be advisable to undertake some background research so that you are aware of referral criteria for relevant hostel providers that you may subsequently consider, assessment processes and how long someone may have to wait for a hostel place, so that you appear knowledgeable. You may have to ask your practice educator for guidance. By having this information to hand you will improve your credibility with your inter-professional colleagues.
- Make an effort to understand your colleagues' perspectives as fully as possible. Margaret, the community mental health nurse, is aware of Andy's parents' views and the carer stress they are under, and also of the severity and long-term nature of Andy's mental health problem – that is why she thinks it is a more complex case than a straightforward referral for hostel accommodation. It would be sensible to let her know you appreciate these factors.
- There is a lot to consider: nevertheless, it is vital not to forget other relevant professional skills, such as responding to referrals promptly and communicating politely about what you are doing on a regular basis.

In relation to communicating with service users, authors such as Koprowska (2014) have provided an extensive discussion of the concept of the 'working alliance'. This has its origins in therapeutic practice, and social work shares certain elements, such as achieving change through the development of constructive, helpful relationships where challenge may be offered to the service user as part of that process. This is aligned to concepts of relationship-based social work (see Trevithick, 2012, and Hennessey, 2011). Working relationships in an inter-professional environment are much more effective when social work and other staff are aware of the relationship dimension of their work with each other. We advocate that time and attention is given to the formation of a positive 'working alliance' (using the skills outlined in Chapter Two), particularly at the initial engagement stage, and arguably throughout the period of contact. This is equally applicable if you are only interacting at set points of contact, such as case reviews or strategy meetings.

LISTENING

Many social workers and social work students pride themselves on having good listening skills (see also Chapter Three). Having a sense of shared purpose or some elements of a shared value base is crucial to ensure professionals are able to listen to one another effectively. It might be assumed that all professionals share a value base to some extent, indeed health care professions and social work are currently regulated by the Health and Care Professions Council, signing up to the same set of requirements (HCPC, 2016b), although this is likely to change in the near future. In our example, both Margaret, the community mental health nurse, and Mike, the social worker, are registered with the HCPC; however, there may be differences in individual professions value bases. For example, Margaret, whilst appreciating patient choice, is also concerned with issues of compliance with the medication regimen. Dr Ahmed is concerned with compliance too and he is also focused on trying to achieve a cure for Andy's diagnosed mental illness – or at least the best control of symptoms that can possibly be achieved. (See Bailey, 2012, and Chapter Three for a fuller discussion of professional value bases.) If you are in the kind of setting that only interacts periodically with professionals from other services, then it is equally important to appreciate possible differences based on variations in value bases.

Organisational and other constraints may affect how well professionals can listen to each other. Some teams can be very busy and they may have to have a stringent system of prioritisation, including separate waiting lists for assessment and subsequent intervention. The person you are trying to refer may not meet the agency's particular threshold for involvement and this may make you feel your concerns are not being listened to. You may be offered 'signposting' instead to services provided by the voluntary or independent sector. Of course, you may also do this too and they may feel as frustrated as you would.

Confidentiality is rightly at the forefront of the practice of all professionals, but sometimes information does need to be shared between professionals and between agencies. In many situations it is good practice and necessary to inform service users and carers about the limits of confidentiality and to seek consent. In some situations, information can be shared without consent or prior notification.

> Sharing of information between practitioners and organisations is essential for effective identification, assessment, risk management and service provision. Fears about sharing information cannot be allowed to stand in the way of the need to safeguard and promote the welfare of children and young people at risk of abuse or neglect. (HM Government, 2015: 13)

This is equally applicable to adult services and is particularly pertinent in safeguarding situations or where there are potential risks to safety. You should ensure you are familiar with and always adhere to your agency's confidentiality and information-sharing policy.

REFLECTIVE TASK 11.5

- How would you articulate the social work value base in relation to Andy?
- What in your opinion are the similarities and differences between the value bases of the professions immediately involved with Andy?
- What about other professions who might become involved – housing providers, housing support workers or advocates to ensure Andy's views are heard?
- How much of this is based on fact, or are you relying on hearsay or stereotypes?
- If so, how could this affect your interactions and what could you do to improve the situation?
- How in practice can you ensure you are taking account of organisational factors and differences in understanding of issues such as confidentiality?

EMPATHY

Although it may be considered an unusual assertion, we would suggest that empathy is also an important feature to ensure effective inter-professional communication. Of course, it is more usually applied to work with service users (see also Chapter Five). Trevithick defines empathy as a process that:

> involves attempting to put ourselves in another person's place, in the hope that we can feel and understand another person's emotions, thoughts, actions and motives. Empathy involves trying to understand, as carefully and sensitively as possible, the nature of another person's experience, their unique point of view and what meaning this conveys for the individual. (Trevithick, 2012: 194)

Practitioners in human services are still human. If professionals take an empathic stance, then they are more likely to grasp the essence of referrals and the person making the referral is also much more likely to feel listened to regarding their concerns. Even if ultimately the referral is not accepted, the professional is unlikely to perceive the interaction as a negative one and be dissuaded from further contact in the future. It is even better if workers could engage in 'preparatory empathy' (Shulman, 2012), as discussed in more detail in Chapter Three, so that they can be suitably prepared to address any interpersonal issues that may arise as a consequence of the referral process. It is well-established that social workers, amongst a number of other professionals, can experience high levels of occupational stress leading to 'burnout' (see Wagaman et al., 2015). In making referrals or initiating contact, you will not necessarily be aware of what is happening for the professional at the other end of the telephone – what is happening in their work or professional life, their workloads, pressures arising from the context in which they work, etc. Clearly, it is up to individual workers to maintain boundaries and only practise when they are capable of performing their duties (HCPC, 2016b); taking care to act according to empathic principles should be beneficial and appropriate in most situations that will be encountered.

CLARIFICATION

Clarification (see also Chapter Four) and the closely related skill of challenging, considered next in this chapter (and in Chapter Six), are perhaps the ones that appear most obvious when considering inter-professional working. They are often the communication skills about which students express most concern. However, both are essential to ensure that the best possible response is made to assess and address the needs of service users and carers. As a student social worker, it is particularly important to engage in clarifying activities, partly to ensure that you receive the correct level of support and supervision to ensure the safety of service users, as specified in paragraph 3 of the *Guidance on Conduct and Ethics for Students* (HCPC, 2016a).

As has been discussed previously, members of different professions bring a range of diverse skills and perspectives, which arise out of profession-specific training and the particular value base that is central to their profession of origin. There may be considerable overlap with other professions, or at least appreciation of what the likely approach will be in an integrated team or a team of people who interact regularly. Despite this, clarification and appropriate challenge may still be necessary and social workers should also welcome being asked for clarification or being challenged.

Referrals across disciplines may make certain assumptions that may or may not be correct. For example, a social worker might refer to a health visitor regarding concerns about a young child's nutrition or weight. This could be the right course of action, but equally, a direct referral to a dietician might be possible and more appropriate. Similarly, a primary school aged child could be referred to a school liaison nurse because of apparent developmental delays – but this might not be the correct pathway. The child might need to be seen first by the general practitioner and there may be a specialist assessment service such as a 'healthy child team' or the child may be referred to a hospital service or a clinical psychologist. With so many possible options, it is hardly surprising that clarification is often necessary, alongside confirmation of key facts or details.

Returning to the case of Andy, examples of possible clarifying questions to ask other professionals might be:

- How do you see the problem? / What has your assessment found? / How urgent do you feel the situation is? (These are generic questions which could be applied to a variety of situations.)
- Could you expand a little on why you think that Andy's moving to a hostel would help?
- You have diagnosed X condition. Could you give me some further details about this? From your perspective, what are the implications of such a condition, so I can make any services made available to Andy fully aware of his needs?
- What did you envisage that our service could offer?
- What has already been tried? What other services have been considered?
- What level of contact will you have with Andy? (Again, this is a widely applicable question.)
- Are Andy and his parents aware of the referral? (Important question regarding confidentiality.)
- What have you told Andy and/or his parents about what is likely to happen next? (This is important for managing the service user and carers' expectations.)

There are other questions you might ask depending on the context of your work. You will note that these questions have a clear purpose and are quite tactfully framed. Despite this, it is still possible that a professional might wonder why you are asking for further information. They might just want you to get on with whatever they have asked you to do. In our example of Andy, there might be the assumption that you should just find a hostel place, but if you are to work in a truly person-centred way, as a priority you will want to ascertain Andy's wishes and also consult with his immediate family.

Clarification may be necessary at any point during a piece of work. If more than one professional is involved with a person or family at the same time, then it will be necessary to liaise and communicate at regular intervals. It can be necessary to check the validity of information provided by the service user and to ensure a consistency of approach. At the end of contact it is necessary to record and explain why contact is ending and to give details where appropriate to other professionals, the service user and/or the carer of sources of further support should this be required.

CHALLENGING

The skill of challenging (see also Chapter Six) may be required at any point during inter-professional working. Many of the open questions suggested as part of the clarification process can also be used as challenges. It is important to remember that the skill of challenging is not as daunting as it would first appear. As Moss notes:

> We need to state at the outset that for all its potentially aggressive potential, challenging as an activity can have quite a different 'feel' to it. It can be subtle or gentle; it can draw on humour or be accomplished non-verbally. Challenging, in other words, can often be achieved elegantly without the confrontation that many people so dislike. (2012: 69)

Like all the other skills discussed in this chapter and in the book overall, the skill of challenging can be practised and improved throughout your career.

Challenging becomes more complex when a more junior member of staff from one profession wishes to challenge someone with apparently higher status or more perceived power within a given situation. However, it is clear that in cases where safety is an issue, you have an overriding duty to act, regardless of concerns about perceived power differentials, as specified by paragraph seven in the Revised *Guidance on Conduct and Ethics for Students*:

> If you are worried about the safety or wellbeing of service users, carers or others, you should speak to an appropriate member of staff at your education provider or practice placement provider promptly. (HCPC, 2016c: 13)

In our example, imagine you need to challenge either Margaret, the community mental health nurse, or Dr Ahmed or even Mike, your practice educator. Your assessment indicates that Andy does not want to move and he has only been neglecting his personal hygiene and isolating himself for a couple of months. He has told you he has been disposing of his medication rather than taking it as prescribed. You feel that there is an issue with medication compliance which your colleagues are not fully aware of and that, in addition, some other methods of helping Andy should be suggested, such as engaging him in activities he might enjoy outside of the home.

REFLECTIVE TASK 11.6

- How would you feel about presenting information that ostensibly more senior colleagues may not be aware of or in agreement with?
- What would you need to do in terms of 'preparatory empathy?' (Understanding the perspectives and agendas of your colleagues in the inter-professional context.)
- In order to convey the outcome of your assessment effectively, what other information might you need to take into account or present?

In any situation, you would need to ascertain how to go about presenting information that might be challenging to your colleagues in the inter-professional team. You may find the following suggestions helpful:

- Think about the implications of how you convey the information. Inter-professional liaison often takes place during formal and informal meetings. These meetings may or may not include service users and carers. It may be necessary to have a pre-meeting meeting to express your opinions. Consider who is present if contentious issues are to be discussed, although this does not mean that you should conceal or avoid issues when they need open discussion.
- A tactful approach, where you clearly demonstrate understanding of your colleagues' perspectives and show that you have taken their views into account, goes a long way.

CASE STUDY 11.1 CONTINUED

Imagine the following scenario. In the weekly inter-professional meeting, you are asked about your assessment of Andy. Reflect on this response:

I've visited Andy twice and he has been happy to speak to me. His room is in a pretty bad state with lots of take-away cartons lying around and he wasn't wearing clean clothes on either occasion, so I can see why I have been asked to get involved. *(You are acknowledging concerns.)* Andy's Dad told me there has been a real change over the last two months and he was fairly sure Andy had stopped his medication. His Mum and Dad are under a lot of pressure *(acknowledging the carer stress aspect)* but they don't really want him to move out and they don't think he does either. They think he needs to get his medication back on track – is that something you could help him with Margaret? *(Recognising that the contribution of another profession would be useful.)* And he would like to get out more and meet people in a safe environment – I could look at that if we agree? *(Making clear what you are going to do.)*

Practise how you might inform the meeting of the outcome of your assessment.

You need to remain true to your social work values – the value bases of your colleagues may vary a little to your own in that different aspects may be emphasised, but you will find that there is common ground. Remember, you need to balance tact and assertiveness to achieve a positive outcome for Andy.

COMMUNICATION SKILLS AUDIT: SKILLS IN INTER-PROFESSIONAL COMMUNICATION

Finally, reflect on your strengths and areas for development in relation to inter-professional communication and identify two or three action points for you to develop (Table 11.1).

Table 11.1   Communication skills audit: skills in inter-professional communication

	Strengths in inter-professional communication	Areas for development	Action points to improve skills in inter-professional communication
Domain 1 Professionalism			
Domain 2 Values and ethics			
Domain 3 Diversity			
Domain 4 Rights and justice			
Domain 6 Critical reflection and analysis			
Domain 7 Intervention and skills			
Domain 8 Contexts and organisations			

CONCLUSION

This chapter has provided an overview of the key communication skills involved in inter-professional work. Inter-professional working places a distinctive set of demands on social workers, as a number of contextual, ethical and organisational issues complicate the situation. There are also possible differences in value bases, perspective, priorities and accountability. Fundamentally, the purpose of inter-professional working is to provide an effective, thorough and safe service to service users and carers. It is argued that communication is key to this process, and that the central communication skills of initial engagement, listening, empathy, clarification and challenging, more commonly discussed in relation to service users and carers, are of equal applicability to professional interactions. Student social workers need to pay close attention to the development of their skills in this area and it is something that qualified workers will also need to focus and reflect on, whichever context they are working in.

However, a final word of warning: do not engage so robustly with professional colleagues that you forget the service user. Pert et al. (2017) found that, albeit small numbers in their research, young people felt excluded from looked-after child meetings, at the expense of inter-professional working. Inter-professional communication should enhance the service user's experience, not diminish their role.

FURTHER READING

Bailey, D. (2012) *Interdisciplinary Working in Mental Health*. Basingstoke, Hampshire: Palgrave Macmillan. Chapter Two provides a useful account of how variations in value bases and preferred models of working affect the inter-disciplinary working context.

Crawford, K. (2012) *Interprofessional Collaboration in Social Work Practice*. London: Sage. Chapter Six considers the specific contribution of the social work profession to inter-disciplinary work and also examines some of the key challenges.

Davis, J.M. and Smith, M. (2012) *Working in Multi-professional Contexts: A Practical Guide for Professionals in Children's Services*. London: Sage. Chapter Two considers the specific case of children's services and demonstrates using practical, hypothetical examples how inter-professional approaches underpin effective practice.

MANAGING ENDINGS

Links to Knowledge and Skills Statements

Adults: person-centred practice; safeguarding; effective assessment; direct work with individuals and families; supervision, critical reflection and analysis; organisational context; professional ethics and leadership

Children's: relationships and effective direct work; communication; adult mental ill health, substance misuse, domestic abuse, physical ill health and disability; analysis, decision making, planning and review; role of supervision; organisational context

INTRODUCTION

This chapter will review the process of managing endings in social work practice by exploring the different ways we can experience endings, as well as encouraging readers to think about what endings may mean for service users. The literature on endings in social work practice is sparse, and thus reveals that this is a neglected side of social science research. Shulman (2016) concurs this may mirror Western society's difficulty at coping with endings in general. Thompson states endings are a very important:

part of the helping process and therefore needs to be handled carefully and sensitively. If it is mishandled, then much of the good work that has previously been done may be undone. (2015a: 247)

Therefore, as a practitioner it is important to allow sufficient time to plan the process of ending working relationships and to understand how endings feature in social work practice.

ENDING AS PART OF INTERVIEWING

Trevithick (2006: 183) discusses ending interviews and makes the distinction between 'uncomplicated and difficult endings'. These describe difficulties in pacing interviews within the allocated time and keeping within this during straightforward encounters. For example, when time is running over and the pressures of other work commitments mean that you need to bring an interview to a tactful closure. This could include reminding the service user of the time remaining for today's discussion and in this time trying to agree goals for the next meeting. Within this preparatory approach towards the closing phase of an interview, the service user should leave the discussion feeling unhurried and clear about when the next visit will take place and what the focus of this will be. Trevithick (2006) refers to last-minute disclosures as more problematic and these usually occur when service users find working to time boundaries difficult and reveal big issues just as we are preparing to leave. She advocates that when under time pressure, a way to respond to such practice encounters would be to acknowledge the impact of the problem and suggests negotiating ending these encounters safely. For example, holding and recognising the emotion of the issue at hand and agreeing to talk again very soon, when sufficient time can be spent to explore these emotions. If someone is very upset and you are concerned about them, Trevithick suggests that the practitioner identifies and finds someone in the personal network who can offer emotional support in the here and now after you leave. Egan provides a pragmatic and realistic reminder of the complexity of helping and human emotions, by saying that at the end of the working relationship 'many client problems are managed or coped with not solved' (2014: 313). Our role is to help people to develop improved strategies to manage problems, to be effective change agents for themselves with renewed skills of resilience to tackle life's setbacks.

ENDINGS AS PART OF FORMAL SYSTEMS AND PROCESSES

Within social work academia and practice, Coulshed and Orme's (1998) writing about endings has endured over time and remains relevant to a contemporary discussion about endings and disengagement. They identified the following eleven reasons why social work practice may end. Some of these examples are natural endings, which can occur in both planned or unexpected ways. There are also more procedural endings that illustrate the bureaucratic demands of working in organisations.

- *Agreed goals*: are achieved within a pre-set time limit and the case is closed.
- *Service user withdraws*: deciding they have been helped enough.
- *Absence*: the social worker leaves their employment, or the service user moves from the district (case transfer, this may include following formal referrals for safety if a child or adult is thought to be at risk).
- *The end of statutory requirements*: a court case, plan of protection, rehabilitation or service discharge results in the ending of a duty to visit.
- *Agency policy on time limits of the work*: some behavioural approaches have fixed end points built into the programme of work.
- *Workload management and priority systems*: the worker's time is required on other priorities.
- *Resource limitations*: there is insufficient or lack of time or services to complete the work.
- *Lack of time and pressure of work:* the work is unfocused, may drift and may gradually come to an end.
- *Death of the service user*: unplanned or expected death can pose difficult emotions and questions for the worker and sometimes the agency if this results in a case review.
- *Advice from supervisor*: may suggest it is time to end the work and reveal this to a worker who is struggling to identify or accept this.
- *Influence of other agencies*: professionals' roles and lines of accountability may change within the context of the work, making disengagement appropriate.

Each of these are examples of the multiple ways in which an ending can occur in social work practice, and they portray the variance of tasks as well as the dynamic and changing nature of practice encounters. Essentially they reveal some of the drivers for change that require the practitioner to be able to adapt and to creatively manage endings by reconciling themselves to the unpredictable nature of practice. Moreover, both Thompson (2015b: 161) and Trevithick (2006: 181) stress the importance of taking a holistic view of practice encounters and Thompson suggests that we should think of this in a systematic focused way. He sees this as a process which has five stages: assessment, intervention, review, ending and evaluation. This model highlights the interconnectness of each phase of the work, which Thompson suggests if done properly provides an opportunity for the practitioner to critically reflect on their personal development.

When discussing endings, many authors (Coulshed and Orme, 1998; Egan, 2014; Moss 2008; Shulman, 2016; Thompson, 2015a) state that practitioner ambivalence and mixed emotions are an expected part of saying goodbye within helping relationships. Moss (2008) emphasises the importance of self-awareness from the practitioner on how they have dealt with endings in their own lives, as these might have been painful or traumatic. Awareness of this can help the practitioner to be prepared for transference of powerful feelings that can come with endings and for some people 'seep into' practice (Moss, 2008: 99).

REFLECTIVE TASK 12.1

Think of an occasion in your life when you have had a good experience of the ending of an important relationship or encounter.

- What are the elements that made this a positive experience?

Next, using an unhappy or negative life experience, what factors made this unsatisfactory?

By completing Reflective task 12.1 you will have begun to locate your own feelings about loss and endings. As the literature suggests, this will largely include ambivalence associated with feelings of a sense of pride for goals attained and self-efficacy, pain, confusion and, for some, abandonment and rejection. We have spent time throughout this book returning to the core theme of self-awareness and emotional intelligence and again this important ability to be attuned to our own emotional state is evident when thinking about endings. Having an awareness of the affective, feeling side of endings is crucial to helping us understand how we can manage these emotions as practitioners. Importantly this self-awareness fundamentally assists us to draw on some of these feelings to gain an understanding of how service users and carers may experience endings. Trevithick (2006) explains that many service users will have had difficult life experiences in relation to crises, trauma and separation, including unresolved losses, associated with being let down and breaches of trust or abuse by people in their lives. These adverse experiences can cause people to find endings challenging, therefore planning a positive ending to the working relationship should be seen as an opportunity to help people experience a good ending and to assist them on how to move on when relationships and support systems change. A person's reaction when endings are introduced to the work can reveal how much they have come to rely on us, and their feelings at the prospect of losing this support can be both overwhelming and frightening. Huntley (2002) suggests that the power of endings can trigger earlier negative attachment behaviours for service users who may react in hostile ways. This could include projecting blame onto the practitioner or regressing backwards in the progress achieved, including repeating the negative behaviours that were the cause of the original concern. Such behaviours could be unconscious attempts to say to the worker, 'You can't leave now, the problem is back!' or 'Go on, leave me – see if I care!' Thus during the process of ending, it is common for the service user to begin to withdraw and miss appointments as a way to adapt to this phase and it can be a signal that they are finding it painful. The challenge for the worker is to introduce this early into the working relationship, and to prepare for this by allowing sufficient time and using 'I' statements to humanise endings, including sharing your feelings about the progress the person has made (Nelson-Jones, 2016).

PREPARING SERVICE USERS AND CARERS FOR ENDINGS

Crompton and Galaway (1994) and Murdin (2000: 3) describe preparation for endings as 'constructive processes', which run throughout the three phases of endings, referral, transfers and terminations. In addressing issues that relate to referral, Crompton and Galaway (1994) state that asking for help is not a straightforward process and is akin to thinking about crisis intervention. Before approaching an agency for help, the service user will likely have used all internal and external strategies they are aware of to try to solve their problem. Additionally, once they have taken the positive step towards asking for help they will often have to navigate their way through bureaucratic systems of social care agencies. This window of opportunity when the service user is open to seeking support is a 'short vulnerable period' (Crompton and Galaway, 1994: 523) and the service user can be left with feelings of desperation if an offer of help is not forthcoming. Crompton and Galaway highlight the importance of referral systems and workers being accountable for humane endings and helpful problem-solving approaches, which allow time to refer on or to signpost the service user to other agencies in a staged way which does not cause distress to the service user.

REFLECTIVE TASK 12.2

Imagine you are shadowing a social worker in a supported housing project, which has strict rules about who can access emergency accommodation, including abstinence from alcohol and drugs. An adult male who is homeless and who admits to using drugs, comes into the agency asking for help. He becomes abusive when the worker tells him he is not eligible for housing. The man becomes tearful and dejected, saying, 'You are all a waste of space and can't help anyone.'

- What alternative approach could you take here, that could be more constructive?
- Think of the verbal messages you would use to show you are willing to support this person?
- Think of some of the practical problem-solving approaches you might try.

The process of case transfer happens when a new worker is absent through illness, resignation or when service responsibilities are transferred across teams. Human nature likes continuity and familiarity and this is particularly relevant when we think about the more intimate aspects of our personal and private lives. For example, if they had a choice most people would value seeing the same health worker/general practitioner (GP) with whom they were familiar because, based on previous encounters, they will have formed a judgement of each other's style, developed some sense of trust and found a way to share personal information.

The same applies to the social worker, who may have spent many hours in a person's home or family group, including sitting at their bedside if they have been unwell or in hospital. The nature of this relational-based practice requires us to work closely in people's spaces and Ferguson terms this closeness as 'intimate practice' (2011: 8). During the transfer of a worker, the departing practitioner needs to manage their own feelings, which may include a feeling that they are abandoning the service user part way through the work. Trust is part of the working relationship and the new worker will need to be mindful of allowing enough time for the service user to work through this loss. Part of this might be seen in acting out or testing behaviours before entering a phase where trust can be attempted again. Good practice should include telling the service about the transfer of a worker as soon as possible, and allowing enough time to introduce the new person and to work through the ideas the person has about how these meetings will go and what the new person will be like. Crompton and Galaway suggest that during the first encounter the new worker is just introduced for five minutes, the second time they sit in and observe the encounter, the third time they work together with the new worker who is 'gradually assuming the primary professional role' (1994: 525) as the goals of work are discussed and new ones set. There may be a final fourth session with time at the end for the first worker to say goodbye. In reality, the time allowed for this may need to be advocated from the worker within the agency's constraints of resources and the pressure to pass on new priorities to the worker during a transfer process.

SAYING GOODBYE: PUTTING THIS INTO PRACTICE

The final stage is evaluating the work which forms part of the termination and disengagement phase. When discussing the subject of reviewing goals within a task-centred approach, Marsh and Doel (2005) make the distinction between reviewing and evaluating if goals have been achieved and reviewing the process of how the work has been met and people's feelings about this. Following these principles is helpful as it reminds workers that evaluation and planned endings are better achieved within an overarching approach of clear focused plans of work. Additionally, Thompson (2015a) cautions that working in an unfocused way, without having an ending in sight, can create a highly pressured and confusing environment for workers: one in which the practitioner does not think deeply about the work they are doing, critically seeking out its purpose and direction. This is likely to cause drift for service users which could be dangerous and lead them to form unhelpful levels of dependency on the worker. For the practitioner as well, losing sight of this drift can cause feelings of demotivation, resulting in emotional exhaustion and 'burn out'. Working in a systematic way provides the benefit of moving the work forwards to realistic conclusions and allows the practitioner to learn about their strengths and what works. Continual evaluation forms part of the ongoing cycle of critical reflection on performance and practice, and is a crucial part of professional development.

Crompton and Galaway (1997) discuss termination or disengagement of the working relationship and the importance of evaluating the intervention within a goal-directed approach which takes precedence. Service users may show that they are ready for the work to finish by taking positive steps to reach their goals independently of the worker. Planning for termination should happen well in advance and be part of the overall contract of the work. This may also include sharing the plans for disengagement with other relevant people in the service user's network, such as family, friends and professionals. As well as direct resistance from the service users, there can also be challenges from this wider network as they reappraise their role in the person's life. This may evoke feelings of fears about what the termination of social work services may mean for them including the need to offer more support (Thompson 2015a). In addition, by not stopping to review goals we may be trying to achieve the impossible as the circumstances will have changed; therefore having clear, focused goals is a significant factor in keeping things on track.

Part of the termination phase allows the practitioner and service user to review the self-sufficiency of the person to 'go it alone'. This includes exploring successes and the skills they now have to manage on their own. As mentioned previously, every person will respond in a unique way towards saying goodbye, and this is usually closely associated with life experiences of losses. Thus the potential for this to cause strong reactions and setbacks remains high. Working with the service user to plan how to say goodbye and having a vision of what the final visit will look like is crucial. Time can be measured and marked on calendars or as the numbering of appointments. The practitioner should provide gentle and regular verbal reminders of how close the work is to achieving the end by saying 'We now have X sessions left'. It is important to symbolically mark the last contact with either a supporting letter or by holding a special event/activity which the service user is involved in choosing. The discussions also needs to include signposting how to access future support and leaving the door open for the future if further help is required. At this stage the social worker may be reflective and have mixed feelings, as they ask, 'Have I done enough, could I have done more?' This process of critical reflection on the work and its progress can cause ambivalent feelings in worker and service user and requires sufficient time to adjust to as the ending is gradually accepted.

There are different ways towards preparing service users for endings. Coulshed and Orme advocate a number of positive strategies, which they term 'gradual withdrawal aids' (1998: 234), which can be adopted. For example, setting realistic objectives during the final weeks for the service user to achieve, to give them a sense of measuring how far they have come in being able to have control over and to direct events in their own lives. Additionally, the gradual withdrawing of social work contacts is phased in, including reducing the frequency of visits and phone calls. In planning endings which include the service user going to live in another location, such as independent living or an adoptive placement, this would include a gradual increase in the time spent in this location with the new family or support team. Clearly such endings as these are delicate and cannot be timetabled to a fixed plan, as they require enough time to begin to transfer attachments, and each person will go through this phase at their own pace. Surprisingly, if effective planning has taken place, in the early stages of moving home, including thorough involvement in decisions about choosing carers, visiting regularly and decorating personal spaces, these moves can happen quite quickly. When the time arrives for the final goodbye, the use of ritual or ceremony to record the ending including photographs or the sharing of a special activity is accepted good practice to enable service users to leave with a positive experience. In children's social work this is commonly expressed in a life-story book, where, as well as recording developmental milestones in a child's life, important events and transitions are captured to help the child remember that they were cared about and valued by professionals. Roberts (2011) conducted research into the experience of short-term foster carers who had gone through endings in seeing children and young people leave their care. This revealed bureaucracy within the social work system which did not allow sufficient time for endings to be planned and found that they often occurred abruptly. Therefore, we end on a note of caution for practitioners to be effective in advocating for sufficient space and time to end the work appropriately.

REFLECTIVE TASK 12.3

Putting endings into practice

You are the social worker for the Marsh family, which consists of Kevin and his children Kala, 8 years old, and Josh, 11 years old. Social care began working with the family several years ago because of concerns about neglect and a lack of appropriate supervision. The children's mother, Marie, was a long-term drug user, and Kevin intermittently left the family home because of arguments with Marie. You have worked with the family for three years and know them well. During that time the parents have separated and Kevin reluctantly became the children's primary carer. Marie now lives in accommodation for the homeless, and through offering support and mediation you have managed to establish supervised contact for the children with their mother. Over time Kevin's confidence as a single carer has increased and the family's circumstances are now stable. Kevin has relied heavily on your visits and usually has a warm and friendly relationship with you. Your manager has said that the case is ready for closure in the next month and when you tell Kevin, he reacts angrily and says your offers to help him have all amounted to 'false promises'.

- Think about the approach you would take to plan a positive ending with this family over the next month.
- Who would you work with and why?
- Which other agencies might be helpful to assist in planning to meet the family's short-term and long-term needs?

It is both okay and emotionally intelligent, to reflect that this will be difficult, both for you and the family. You have developed a working relationship, one that has adhered to professional boundaries, yet one that has utilised trust and commitment. By acknowledging and addressing the relationship, you can support Kevin to identify the strengths that he has developed, whilst empowering him to parent independently without your support.

COMMUNICATION SKILLS AUDIT: MANAGING ENDINGS

Finally, reflect on your strengths and areas for development in relation to managing endings and identify two or three action points for you to develop (Table 12.1).

Table 12.1   Communication skills audit: managing endings

	Strengths in planning ending your work with service users	Areas for development	Action points to improve your ability to model positive endings
Domain 1 Professionalism			
Domain 3 Diversity			
Domain 5 Knowledge			
Domain 6 Critical reflection and analysis			
Domain 7 Intervention and skills			
Domain 8 Contexts and organisations			

CONCLUSION

This chapter has discussed aspects of social work practice and tasks that constitute an ending or major change in the professional relationship. The feelings and processes that are present for both worker and service user have been reviewed to allow practitioners to ensure sufficient time is given to plan positive endings so that the person's achievements and progress is sustained and valued. We have reviewed strategies for managing time during day-to-day encounters to respond sensitively to endings whilst keeping the work within agreed boundaries of the working contract. Additionally, we have explained the gradual process of withdrawal and considered some good practice examples of how to apply these to plan positive endings, including the use of celebration, ritual and continuous professional development. Through utilising the support of colleagues and supervisors you should be able to approach endings in an informed way and to reflect on how you felt about these practice encounters. This will enable you to learn from each ending, increase your own levels of resilience and give you the confidence to model positive endings when they are happening in service users' lives.

FURTHER READING

Shulman, L. (2016) *The Skills of Helping Individual, Families, Groups and Communities*, 8th edn. Boston, MA: Cengage Learning. Chapter Six, 'Endings and transitions', provides therapeutic insight into the need for positive endings for service users to ensure that successful interventions can be utilised post intervention.

Thompson, N. (2015) *People Skills*. Basingstoke, Hampshire: Palgrave Macmillan. Chapter Twenty-Eight, 'Ending', stimulates reflection on the need for positive endings within social work to ensure person-centred transitions.

CONCLUSION

This book has worked with you through the different communication skills you will need as a student and progressing on as a qualified social worker. It has supported you to develop as a self-aware, reflective practitioner who is able to recognise both your strengths and areas for development to enhance your communication skills. It has encouraged you to identify the communicator that *you* are: to utilise your natural communication skills, harness and enhance them to maximise your engagement with service users, carers, family members and professionals alike.

In order to engage service users, you will have developed your skills in relation to initial engagement, listening, empathy, clarification and challenging. You will have developed a sense of the difficult balance needed by social work communicators for an open and honest working relationship that is both person-centred and agency-procedure focused; that is at the same time both empathic and challenging; that is proactive in facilitating change within often restrictive confines; that is creative and flexible yet procedural; and that takes account of the issues of power and control that a statutory social worker wields in a sensitive yet assertive manner that is challenging of oppressive practice, by service users, society and service provision. None of these are simple skills, and you should now understand the complexity of communication required by the social worker.

Furthermore, you will have also seen that communication is not limited to these skills, but that you will need to apply these core communication skills to written communication and communication with other professionals to ensure that you are most effective in supporting your service user. Tact and assertiveness are critical skills, which as an inter-professional communicator, enable you to advocate the service user's and service provision's needs and priorities, whilst listening to others enables you to make informed holistic decisions. Written communication should be concise and clear to ensure that your message is understood by the reader.

It can be seen, throughout the book, that a strong social work communicator employs a wide range of skills to engage a service user to achieve change. You will have developed your verbal and non-verbal communication skills, considered the impact of *self* on the communication with the service user and the impact of the service user's immediate and longer-term history on their communication skills, to enhance your emotional intelligence, and developed your confidence to undertake tactful and assertive interventions with service users. By undertaking the activities throughout each chapter, you will have practised and developed the relevant skills. This should be supplemented by university teaching, practical experience in your placement, and also your job and/or social relationships, and by generic university resources, for example that your university library may provide.

We hope that you have also developed your emotional intelligence, resilience, sense of social work identity and ability to reflect whilst working through the book. The verbal and non-verbal communication are like the top half of a swan: graceful and effective. Underneath this, emotional intelligence, identity and reflection steer and power your communication as does a swan's feet. An awareness of your strengths and vulnerabilities will support your ability to communicate effectively, and an awareness of the service user's needs will inform your individualised responses, meaning that your emotional intelligence will enhance and direct your communication techniques. Furthermore, by reflecting on all your interventions and communications you will be able to recognise good practice and continue to use it, and recognise where you could enhance your practice from less productive communications and develop stronger techniques. We would remind you that social communication requires a range of styles, that one size does not fit all, and that different communication styles will be required for different service users or even with the same service user at different times in your intervention. Work out your preferred, and most effective, style of communication, but also be flexible and responsive to the service user's need.

A FINAL REFLECTIVE TASK

Reflect on your communication strengths that you have developed through exploring the book. List the three best communication assets that you feel that you now have, and three areas that you would most like to develop as you progress through your social work journey (Table C.1).

Table C.1 Communication skills audit: ongoing development

Strengths in communication	Areas for development	Action points to improve communication skills

This exercise is aimed to support you to reflect on your progress throughout the journey that you have undertaken. Compare your areas for development in the early chapters, with these strengths: you have made progress by reflecting on your skills and practising new techniques. But social work skills development never ends. The Professional Capability Framework (BASW, 2016) is clear that professional development is an on going task for all social workers, from your first day as a social work student, to the heady heights of assistant director. At the stage that you begin your career as a qualified social worker, you will be assessed utilising the Knowledge and Skills Statements (Department for Education, 2016; Department of Health, 2015). The skills that you have learnt throughout this book will enhance your ability to meet each of these statements. Relationships, direct work and communication are a social worker's fundamental skills, each of which is embedded in the Knowledge and Skills Statements. As you develop as a qualified social worker you will pull on the core skills outlined throughout this book. These skills will enable you to undertake the often complex and challenging tasks that are asked of you. For example, giving evidence in court involves communicating using your listening skills with emotional intelligence to hear questions and answering in a clear, empathic manner, pulling on strong written evidence, albeit in a formal setting. As you finish the book, irrespective of the stage you are now at, identifying the communication skills that you need to continue to develop will enable you to continue your continuing professional development as a student and qualified social worker.

We hope that this is that start, not the end, of your communication skills development, and that you will continue to reflect and enhance your skills as you progress through your social work career. Good luck.

Paula, Mary and Melanie

BIBLIOGRAPHY

Adebowale, Lord V. (2013) *Report into Mental Health and Policing in London*. London: HMSO.

Anthony, W.A. (1993) Recovery from mental illness: the guiding vision of the mental health service system in the 1990s. *Psychosocial Rehabilitation Journal*, 16(4): 11–23.

AS *v* TH (False Allegations of Abuse) [2016] EWHC 532 Fam.

Bailey, D. (2012) *Interdisciplinary Working in Mental Health*. Basingstoke, Hampshire: Palgrave Macmillan.

Bamford, T. (1990) *The Future of Social Work*. Basingstoke: Macmillan.

Banks, S. (2009) Professional values and accountabilities, in R. Adams (ed.) *Critical Practice in Social Work*. Basingstoke, Hampshire: Palgrave Macmillan, pp. 32–7.

Bassot, B. (2016) *The Reflective Journal*. London: Palgrave.

Baum, N. (2017) Gender-sensitive intervention to improve work with fathers in child welfare services. *Child and Family Social Work*, 2017: 419–27.

BASW (2016) *Professional Capabilities Framework*. Available at: www.basw.co.uk/pcf/ (accessed 15 March 2017).

Beck, E., Kropf, N. and Blume, L.P. (2010) *Social Work and Restorative Justice: Skills for Dialogue, Peace-making and Resolution*. Oxford: Oxford University Press.

Beresford, P., Croft, S. and Adshead, L. (2008) 'We don't see her as a social worker': a service user case study of the importance of the social worker's relationship and humanity. *British Journal of Social Work*, 38: 1388–1407.

Borg, J., Lantz, A. and Gulliksen, J. (2015) Accessibility to electronic communication for people with cognitive disabilities: a systematic search and review of empirical evidence. *Universal Access in the Information Society*, 14(4): 547–62.

Brammer, A. (2014) *Social Work Law*. Essex: Pearson Education.

Cameron, A., Lart, R., Bostock, L, and Coomber, C. (2013) Factors that promote and hinder joint and integrated working between health and social care services. *SCIE Research Briefing* 41. Available at: www.scie.org.uk/publication/briefings/briefing41.

Children and Social Work Bill (HL Bill 57). Available at: www.publications.parliament.uk/pa/bills/lbill/2016-2017/0057/lbill_2016-20170057_en_1.htm (accessed 20 July 2016).

Christiansen, A. and Roberts, K. (2005) Integrating health and social care assessment and care management; findings from a pilot project evaluation. *Primary Health Care Research and Development*, 6(3): 1297–305.

Clapson, A. (2016) So how biased are you? *Professional Social Work*, May: 14–15.

Clark, A. (2007) *Empathy in Counselling and Psychotherapy: Perspectives and Practices*. Princeton, NJ: Lawrence Erlbaum.

Crompton, B.R. and Galaway, B. (1994*) Social Work Processes*. California: Brooks/Cole.

Constable, G. (2013) *Skills for Social Work Practice*. London: Sage.

Coulshed, V. and Orme, J. (1998) *Social Work Practice: An Introduction*. Basingstoke, Hampshire: Palgrave Macmillan.

Craig, S.L. and Muskat, B. (2013) Bouncers, brokers and glue: the self-described roles of social workers in urban hospitals. *Health and Social Work*, 38(1): 7–16.

Crawford, K. (2012) *Interprofessional Collaboration in Social Work Practice*. London: Sage.

Davis, J.M. and Smith, M. (2012) *Working in Multi-professional Contexts: A Practical Guide for Professional in Children's Services*. London: Sage.

De Shazer, S. (1984) The death of resistance. *Family Process*, 23: 79–93.

De Shazer, S. (1985) *Keys to Solution in Brief Therapy*. New York: Norton.

Deegan, P.E. (1988) Recovery: the lived experience of rehabilitation. *Psychosocial Rehabilitation Journal*, 11(4): 11–19.

Department for Education (2015) *Working Together to Safeguard Children: A Guide to Inter-agency Working to Safeguard and Promote the Welfare of Children*. London: HMSO.

Department for Education (2016) *Knowledge and Skills for Child and Family Social Work*. Available at: www.gov.uk/government/uploads/system/uploads/attachment_data/file/524743/Knowledge_and_skills_statement_for_approved_child_and_family_practitioners.pdf (accessed 15 March 2017).

Department of Health (2000) *Framework for the Assessment of Children in Need and their Families*. Norwich: HMSO.

Department of Health (2001) *Valuing People: A New Strategy for Learning Disability in the 21st Century*. Norwich: HMSO.

Department of Health (2010) *Valuing People Now*. Norwich: HMSO.

Department of Health (2015) *Knowledge and Skills Statement for Social Workers in Adult Services*. Available at: www.gov.uk/government/uploads/system/uploads/attachment_data/file/411957/KSS.pdf (accessed 15 March 2017).

Doel, M. and Marsh, P. (1992) *Task-Centred Social Work*. Abingdon: Routledge.

Dominelli, L. (2009) Values in critical practice: contested entities with enduring qualities, in R. Adams (ed.) *Critical Practice in Social Work*. Basingstoke, Hampshire: Palgrave Macmillan, pp. 19–29.

Doran, G.T. (1981) There's a S.M.A.R.T. way to write management's goals and objectives. *Management Review, AMA FORUM*, 70(11): 35–36.

Driscoll, J. (ed.) (2007) *Practising Clinical Supervision: A Reflective Approach for Healthcare Professionals*. Edinburgh: Balliere Tindall.

Dunhill, A. (2010) What is communication? The process of transferring information, in A. Dunhill, B. Elliott and A. Shaw (eds) *Effective Communication with Children and Young People, their Families and Carers*. Exeter: Learning Matters.

Dyke, C. (2016) *Writing Analytical Assessments in Social Work*. Northwich: Critical Publishing.

East Riding Safeguarding Children Board (2013) Serious case review relating to a young person who died at the age of fourteen. Available at: www.erscb.org.uk/EasySiteWeb/GatewayLink.aspx?alId=200833 (accessed 11 April 2017).

Egan, G. (2002) *The Skilled Helper*, 7th edn. Belmont, CA: Brooks Cole.

Egan, G. (2014) *The Skilled Helper: A Client-centred Approach,* 10th edn. Hampshire: Cenage Learning.

Ekman, P. (2004) *Emotions Revealed: Understanding Faces and Feelings*. Phoenix, NJ: Phoenix Press.

Elhai, J. and Hall, B. (2015) How secure is mental health providers' electronic patient communication? An empirical investigation. *Professional Psychology: Research and Practice*, 46(6): 444–50.

Fell, B. and Fell, P. (2014) Welfare across borders: a social work process with adult asylum seekers. *British Journal of Social Work*, 44: 1322–39.

Ferguson, H. (2011) *Child Protection Practice*. Basingstoke, Hampshire: Palgrave Macmillan.

Ferguson, H. (2016) What social workers do in performing child protection work: evidence from research into face-to-face practice. *Child & Family Social Work*, 21(3): 283–94.

Fisher, M. (2016) The Social Care Institute for Excellence and Evidence-based Policy and Practice. *British Journal of Social Work*, 46(2): 498–513.

Fleming, N. (1987) *VARK: A Guide to Learning Styles*. Available at: http://vark-learn.com (accessed 15 March 2017).

Fook, J. (2016) *Social Work: A Critical Approach to Practice*. London: Sage.

Forrester, D. and Harwin, J. (2006) Parental substance misuse and child care social work: findings from the first stage of a study of 100 families. *Child and Family Social Work*, 11: 325–35.

Forrester, D., McCambridge, J., Waissbein, C., Emlyn-Jones, R. and Rollnick, S. (2008) Child risk and parental resistance: can motivational interviewing improve the practice of child and family social workers in working with parental alcohol misuse? *British Journal of Social Work*, 38(7): 1302–19.

Francis, L., Holmvall, C. and O'Brien, L. (2015) The influence of workload and civility of treatment on the perpetration of email incivility. *Computers in Human Behaviour*, 46: 191–201.

Freud, S. (1923). The ego and the id. *Internationaler Psycho-analytischer Verlag* (Vienna), W. W. Norton & Company, April 1923.

Frith, L. and Martin, R. (2015) *Professional Writing Skills for Social Workers*. Maidenhead: Open University Press.

Frost, N., Abbott, S. and Race, T. (2015) *Family Support*. Cambridge: Polity.

Gardener, F. (2014) *Being Critically Reflective*. Basingstoke, Hampshire: Palgrave Macmillan.

Gast, L. and Bailey, M. (2014) *Mastering Communication in Social Work*. London: Jessica Kingsley.

Gibbs, G. (1988) *Learning by Doing: A Guide to Teaching and Learning Methods*. Oxford: Further Education Unit. Oxford Polytechnic.

Gibson, N. (2014) Person-centred planning and personalisation, in J. Lishman (ed.) *Social Work and Introduction*. London: Sage, pp. 295–307.

Goleman, D. (1995) *Emotional Intelligence*. New York: Bantam Books.

Grant, L. (2014) Hearts and minds: aspects of empathy and wellbeing in social work students. *Social Work Education*, 33(3): 338–52.

Grant, L. and Brewer, B. (2014) Critical reflection and reflective supervision, in L. Grant and G. Kinman (eds) *Developing Resilience for Social Work Practice*. London: Palgrave Macmillan.

Grant, L. and Kinman, G. (2012) Enhancing wellbeing in social work students: building resilience in the next generation. *Social Work Education*, 31(5): 605–21.

Grant, L. and Kinman, G. (eds) (2014) *Developing Resilience for Social Work Practice*. London: Palgrave Macmillan.

Grant, L., Kinman, G. and Alexander, K. (2014) What's all this about emotion? Developing emotional intelligence in social work students. *Social Work Education*, 33(7): 874–89.

Greer, J. (2016) *Resilience and Personal Effectiveness for Social Workers*. London: Sage.

Gridley, K., Brooks, J. and Glendinning, C. (2014) Good practice in social care: the views of people with severe and complex needs and those who support them. *Health and Social Care in the Community*, 22(6): 588–97.

Hall, C. and Slembrouck, S. (201) Advice giving, in C. Hall, K. Juhila, M. Matarese and C. Van Nijnatten (eds) *Analysing Social Work Communication*. Oxon: Routledge, pp. 98–107.

HCPC (2016a) *Guidance on Conduct and Ethics for Students*. London: HCPC. Available at: www.hcpc.org.uk/assets/documents/10002C16Guidanceonconductandethicsforstudents.pdf (accessed 15 March 2017).

HCPC (2016b) *Standards of Conduct, Performance and Ethics*. London: HCPC. Available at: www.hpc-uk.org/aboutregistration/standards/standardsofconductperformanceand ethics/ (accessed 15 March 2017).

Healy, K. (2014) *Social Work Theories in Context Creating Frameworks for Practice*. Basingstoke, Hampshire: Palgrave.

Healy, K. and Mulholland, J. (2012) *Writing Skills for Social Workers*. London: Sage.

Healy, K., Harrison, G., Venables, J. and Bosly, F. (2016) Collaborating with families in differential responses: practitioners' views. *Child and Family Social Work*, 21(3): 328–38.

Henderson, K. and Mathew-Byrne, J. (2016) Developing communication and interviewing skills, in K. Davies and R. Jones (eds) *Skills for Social Work Practice*. London: Palgrave Macmillan.

Hennessey, R. (2011) *Relationship Skills in Social Work*. London: Sage.

HM Government (2007) *Putting People First. A Shared Vision and Commitment to the Transformation of Adult Social Care*. Norwich: HMSO.

HM Government (2015) *Information Sharing: Advice for Practitioners Providing Safeguarding Services to Children, Young People Parents and Carers*. Available at: www.gov.uk/government/uploads/system/uploads/attachment_data/file/419628/Information_sharing_advice_safeguarding_practitioners.pdf (accessed 15 March 2017).

Honey, P. and Mumford, A. (1982) *Manual of Learning Styles*. London: P Honey.

Hopkins, B. (ed.) (2016) *Restorative Theory in Practice*. London: Jessica Kingsley Publishers.

Horwath, J. (2016) The toxic duo: the neglected practitioner and a parent who fails to meet the needs of their child. *British Journal of Social Work*, 46(6): 1602–16.

Horwath, J. and Tarr, S. (2015) Child visibility in cases of chronic neglect: implications for social work. *British Journal of Social Work*, 45: 1379–94.

Howe, D. (2008) *The Emotionally Intelligent Social Worker*. Basingstoke, Hampshire: Palgrave Macmillan.

Howe, D. (2013) *Empathy. What is it and Why it Matters*. Basingstoke, Hampshire: Palgrave Macmillan

Huntley, M. (2002) Relationship based social work – how do endings impact on the client? *Practice*, 14: 59–66

Ingram, R. (2013) Locating emotional intelligence at the heart of social work practice. *British Journal of Social Work*, 43: 987–1004.

Ingram, R. (2015) *Understanding Emotions in Social Work*. Maidenhead: Open University Press.

Isle of Wight LSCB (2014) Serious case review Baby Z. Available at: www.westsussexscb.org.uk/wp-content/uploads/Isle-of-Wight-Baby-Z.pdf (accessed 15 March 2017).

Jenney, A., Mishna, F., Alaggia, R. and Scott, K. (2014) Doing the right thing? (Re)Considering risk assessment and safety planning in child protection work with domestic violence cases. *Children and Youth Services Review*, 47(1): 92–101.

Juhila, K. (2013) Resistance, in C. Hall, K. Juhila, M. Matarese, and C. Van Nijnatten (eds) *Analysing Social Work Communication*. Oxon: Routledge, pp. 117–36.

Keeling, J and van Wormer, K. (2012) Social worker interventions in situations of domestic violence: what we can learn from survivors' personal narratives? *British Journal of Social Work*, 42: 1354–70.

Kharicha, K., Iliffe, S., Levin, E., Davey, B. and Fleming, C. (2005) Tearing down the Berlin wall: social workers' perspectives on joint working with general practice. *Family Practice*, 22(4): 399–405.

Klin, C., Gunraj, D., Drumm-Hewitt, A., Dashow, E. and Upadhyay, S. (2015) Texting insincerely: the role of the period in text messaging. *Computers in Human Behavior*, 55: 1067–75.

Knott, C. (2013) Reflective practice revisited, in C. Knott and T. Scragg (eds) *Reflective Practice in Social Work*. London: Sage.

Kolb, D.A. (1984) *Experiential Learning: Experience as the Source of Learning and Development* (Vol. 1). New Jersey: Prentice-Hall.

Kolb, D. (2015) *Experiential Learning: Experience as the Source of Learning and Development*, 2nd edn. New Jersey: Pearson.

Konrath, S., Falk, E., Fuhrel-Forbis, A., Liu, M., Swain, J., Tolman, R., Cunningham, R. and Walton, M. (2015) Can text messages increase empathy and prosocial behavior? The development and initial validation of text to connect. *PLoS ONE*, 10(9): 1–27.

Koprowska, J. (2014) *Communication and Interpersonal Skills in Social Work*. London: Sage.

Laird, S. (2014) Training social workers to effectively manage aggressive parental behaviour in child protection in Australia, the United States and the United Kingdom. *British Journal of Social Work*, 44: 1967–83.

Laming, Lord (2003) *The Victoria Climbié Enquiry*. Norwich: HMSO.

Laming, W.H. (2009) *The Protection of Children in England: A Progress Report (The Laming Report)*. London: HMSO.

Levy, D., Shlomo, S. and Itzhaky, H. (2014) The 'building blocks' of professional identity among social work graduates. *Social Work Education*, 33(6): 744–59.

Lishman, J. (2009) *Communication in Social Work*. Basingstoke, Hampshire: Palgrave Macmillan.

Littlechild, B. (2003) Working with aggressive and violent parents in child protection social work. *Social Work in Action*, 15(1): 33–44.

Llewellyn, A., Agu, L. and Mercer, D. (2015) *Sociology for Social Workers*. Cambridge: Polity Press.

Mainstone, F. (2014) *Mastering Whole Family Assessment in Social Work*. London: Jessica Kingsley.

Maiter, S., Alaggia, R., Chan, A. and Leslie, B. (2017) Trial and error: attending to language barriers in child welfare service provision from the perspective of frontline workers. *Child and Family Social Work*, 22(1): 165–74.

Mantell, A. (ed.) (2013) *Skills for Social Work Practice*. London: Sage.

Marsh, P. and Doel, M. (2005) *The Task Centred Book*. Oxfordshire: Routledge.

Masocha, S. (2015) Construction of the 'other' in social workers' discourses of asylum seekers. *Journal of Social Work*, 15(6): 569–85.

McCray, J. (2009) *Nursing and Multi-Professional Practice*. London: Sage.

McLeod, A. (2006) Respect or empowerment? Alternative understandings of 'listening' in childcare social work. *Adoption and Fostering*, 30(4): 43–52.

McNicoll, A. (2016) Judge slams deficient social work assessment in 'extraordinary' case. *Community Care*, 28 June. Available at: www.communitycare.co.uk/2016/06/28/judge-slams-deficient-social-work-assessment-extraordinary-case/ (accessed 15 March 2017).

Miehls, D. and Moffatt, K. (2000) Constructing social work identity based on the reflective self. *British Journal of Social Work*, 30(3): 339–48.

Morrison, D. (2016) Being with uncertainty: a reflective account of a personal relationship with an asylum seeker/refugee. *Counselling Psychology Review*, 31(2): 10–21.

Moss, B. (2008) *Communication Skills for Health and Social Care*. London: Sage.

Moss B. (2012) *Communication Skills in Health and Social Care*, 2nd edn. London: Sage.

Mumby, J. (2016) In the Matter of D (A Child)(no.3). Available at: www.judiciary.gov.uk/wp-content/uploads/2016/01/re-d-a-child-3.pdf (accessed 15 March 2017).

Munford, R. and Sanders, J. (2016) Understanding service engagement: young people's experience of service use. *Journal of Social Work*, 16(3): 283–302.

Munro, E. (2011) *Munro Review of Child Protection: A Child Centred System*. London: Department for Education, HMSO.

Murdin, L. (2000) *How Much is Enough? Endings in Psychotherapy and Counselling*. London: Routledge.

Murray, S. and Humphreys, C. (2014) 'My life's been a total disaster but I feel privileged': care-leavers' access to personal records and their implications for social work practice. *Child & Family Social Work*, 19(2): 215–24.

Myers, S. (2008) Revisiting Lancaster: more things that every social work student should know. *Social Work Education*, 27: 203–11.

National Audit Office (2017) *Health and Social Care Integration*. Available at: www.nao.org.uk/wp-content/uploads/2017/02/Health-and-social-care-integration.pdf (accessed 15 March 2017).

Nelson-Jones, R. (2016) *Basic Counselling Skills: A Helper's Manual*. London: Sage.

Neumann, D.L., Boyle, G.J. and Chan, R.C.K. (2013) Empathy towards individuals of the same and different ethnicity when depicted in negative and positive contexts. *Personality and Individual Differences*, 55(1): 8–13.

Newhill, C.E. and Wexler, S. (1997) Client violence toward children and youth services social workers. *Children and Youth Services Review*, 19(3): 195–212.

NHS (2005) *National Statistics: Adults with Learning Difficulties in England (2003–2004)*. Available at: http://content.digital.nhs.uk/catalogue/PUB01760 (accessed 15 March 2017).

Nicolas, J. (2015) *Conducting the Home Visit in Child Protection*. Maidenhead: Open University Press.

O'Brien, E. (2016) *Psychology for Social Work*. London: Palgrave Macmillan.

O'Rourke, L. (2010) *Recording in Social Work*. London: Policy Press.

Ofsted (2015a) What adults told us were areas for improvement for children's homes, fostering services and adoption services. Available at: www.slideshare.net/Ofstednews/what-adults-told-us-were-areas-for-improvement-for-childrens-homes-fostering-services-and-adoption-services (accessed 15 March 2017).

Ofsted (2015b) What children and young people living in children's homes or with foster carers told us was most important to them. Available at: www.slideshare.net/Ofstednews/what-children-and-young-people-living-in-childrens-homes-or-with-foster-carers-told-us-was-most-important-to-them (accessed 15 March 2017).

Ofsted (2015c) *The Quality of Assessment for Children in Need of Help*. Ofsted, Manchester

Oliver, M. (1983) *Social Work with Disabled People*. Basingstoke: Macmillan.

Oliver, M. (2013) The social model of disability 30 years on. *Disability and Society*, 28(7): 1024–6.

Oliver, M., Sapey, B. and Thomas, P. (2012) *Social Work with Disabled People*, 4th edn (Kindle). Basingstoke: Palgrace Macmillan.

Oxfordshire LSCB (2014) Serious case review Child H. Available at: www.oscb.org.uk/wp-content/uploads/Child-H-Overview-Report-Sept-20141.pdf (accessed 19 March 2017).

Peck, E., Towell, D. and Gulliver, P. (2001) The meaning of culture in health and social care: a case study of the combined trust in Somerset. *Journal of Interprofessional Care*, 15(4): 319–27.

Pennell, J. and Koss, M.P. (2011) Feminist perspectives on family rights: social work and restorative justice processes to stop women abuse, in E. Beck, N. Kropf and P. Leonard (eds) *Social Work and Restorative Justice: Skills for Dialogue, Peacemaking, and Reconciliation*. New York: Oxford University Press, pp. 195–219.

Pert, H., Diaz, C. and Thomas, N. (2017) Children's participation in LAC reviews. *Child and Family Social Work*, 22.

Plafky, C. (2016) From neuro scientific research findings to social work practice: a critical description of the knowledge utilisation process. *British Journal of Social Work*, 46(6): 1502–19.

Prochaska, J. and DiClemente, C. (1983) Stages and processes of self-change in smoking: toward an integrative model of change. *Journal of Consulting and Clinical Psychology*, 5: 390–5.

Ridley, J., Larkins, C., Farrelly, N., Hussein, S., Austerberry, H., Manthorpe, J. and Stanley, N. (2016) Investing in the relationship: practitioners' relationships with looked-after children and care leavers. *Social Work Practices Child and Family Social Work*, 21(1): 55–64.

Roberts, L. (2011) Ending care relationships. Carer perspectives on managing 'endings' within a part-time fostering service. *Adoption & Fostering*, 35(4): 20–28.

Rogers, C. (1967) *On Becoming a Person: A Therapist's View of Psychotherapy*. London: Constable.

Rogers, M., Whitaker, D., Edmondson, D. and Peach, D. (2016) *Developing Skills for Social Work Practice*. London: Sage.

Sawrikar, P. (2013) How effective do families of non–English-speaking background (NESB) and child protection caseworkers in Australia see the use of interpreters? A qualitative study to help inform good practice principles. *Child and Family Social Work*, 20(4): 396–406.

Schön, D. (1983) *The Reflective Practitioner*. London: Maurice Temple Smith.

Scragg, T. (2006) An evaluation of integrated team management. *Journal of Integrated Care*, 14(3): 39–48.

Scragg, T. (2014) Reflective practice, in A. Mantell (ed.) *Skills for Social Work Practice*. London: Sage, pp. 3–19.

Shell, R. (2006) *Bargaining for Advantage*. New York: Penguin Books

Shulman, L. (2012) *The Skills of Helping Individuals, Families, Groups and Communities*, 7th edn. CA: Thomson Brookes Cole.

Shulman, L. (2016) *The Skills of Helping Individuals, Families, Groups and Communities*, 8th edn. Boston, MA: Cengage Learning.

Smale, G., Tuson, G., Biehal, N. and Marsh, P. (1993) Empowerment, assessment, care management and the skilled worker. London: HMSO.

Suoninen, E. and Jokinen, A. (2005) Persuasion in social work interviewing. *Qualitative Social Work*, 4: 469–87.

Sutton, C. (1994) *Social Work, Community Work and Psychology*. Leicester: BPS Books.

Tanner, D., Glasby, J. and McIver, S. (2015) Understanding and improving older people's experiences of service transitions: implications for social work. *British Journal of Social Work*, 45(7): 2056–71.

Tarleton, B. (2015) A few steps along the road? Promoting support for parents with learning difficulties. *British Journal of Learning Disabilities*, 43: 114–20.

Tavormina, M. and Clossey, L. (2017) Exploring crisis and its effects on workers in child protective services work. *Child and Family Social Work*, 2(1): 126–36.

Taylor, B. (2011) *Working with Aggression and Resistance in Social Work*. Exeter: Learning Matters.

Thompson, N. (1997) *Anti-discriminatory Practice*. Basingstoke, Hampshire: Palgrave Macmillan.

Thompson, N. (2011) *Effective Communication*, 2nd edn. Basingstoke, Hampshire: Palgrave Macmillan.

Thompson, N. (2015a) *People Skills*. Basingstoke, Hampshire: Palgrave Macmillan.

Thompson, N. (2015b) *Understanding Social Work*. Basingstoke, Hampshire: Palgrave Macmillan.

Trevithick, P. (2006) *Social Work Skills: A Practice Handbook*. Maidenhead: Open University Press.

Trevithick, P. (2011) Understanding defences and defensiveness in social work. *Journal of Social Work Practice*, 25(4): 389–412.

Trevithick, P. (2012) *Social Work Skills and Knowledge: A Practice Handbook*. Maidenhead: McGraw Hill.

Trotter, C. (2006) *Working with Involuntary Clients: A Guide to Practice*. London: Sage.

Van Berkhout, E. and Malouff, J. (2016) The efficacy of empathy training: a meta-analysis of randomized controlled trials. *Journal of Counselling Psychology*, 63: 32–41.

Wachtel, T. (2005) The next step: developing restorative communities. Paper presented at the Seventh International Conference on Conferencing, Circles and other Restorative Practices, November 2005, Manchester, UK.

Wachtel, T. and McCold, P. (2001) Restorative justice in everyday life, in H. Strang and J. Braithwaite. *Restorative Justice and Civil Society*. Cambridge: Cambridge University Press, pp. 114–129.

Wagaman, A., Geiger, J., Shockley, C. and Segal, E. (2015) The role of empathy in burnout, compassion satisfaction, and secondary traumatic stress among social workers. *Social Work*, 60(3): 201–9.

Warrener, J. (2014) *A Look 'Behind the Curtains' at Personality Disorder and Mental Health Social Work: Perspectives and Expectations of Service Users and Practitioners*. Hertfordshire: University of Hertfordshire.

Whittaker, A. and Havard, T. (2016) Defensive practice as 'fear-based' practice: social work's open secret? *British Journal of Social Work*, 46(5): 1158–74.

Williams, P. and Evans, M. (2013) *Social Work with People with Learning Difficulties*. London: Sage.

Woodcock Ross, J. (2016) *Specialist Communication Skills for Social Workers*. London: Palgrave Macmillan.

Yura, H. and Walsh, M. (eds) (1967) *The Nursing Process: Assessing, Planning, Implementing, and Evaluating*. Washington: Catholic University of America Press.

INDEX

The letter '*b*' after a page number indicates bibliographical information in a Further Reading section.